BENJAMIN LLOYD'S
HYMN BOOK

Benjamin Lloyd

BENJAMIN LLOYD'S HYMN BOOK

A PRIMITIVE BAPTIST SONG TRADITION

CONTAINING ESSAYS AND A COMPACT DISC ILLUSTRATING THE HISTORY OF *THE PRIMITIVE HYMNS* AND THE VARIETY OF WAYS IN WHICH PRIMITIVE BAPTISTS SING FROM THIS WORD-ONLY HYMN BOOK.

EDITED BY JOYCE H. CAUTHEN

"...I have made preliminary arrangements for the publication of a Hymn Book adapted to the use of the Old School Baptists....The Hymns will be classified and embodied under appropriate heads, adapted to singing on all occasions. And in presenting the contemplated work to the public, I do not expect to excel others who have made similar publications; but that duty has for some time rested with weight on my mind, seeing that no one of the Primitive denomination had stepped forward...."

—Benjamin Lloyd, 1841

ALABAMA FOLKLIFE ASSOCIATION
MONTGOMERY, ALABAMA

NATIONAL
ENDOWMENT
FOR THE ARTS

Publication of this work was supported in part by the National Endowment for the Arts and the Folklife Program of the Alabama State Council on the Arts.

Library of Congress Cataloging-in-Publication Data

Benjamin Lloyd's hymn book: a primitive Baptist song tradition /
edited by Joyce H. Cauthen.
P. cm.
Includes bibliographical references and index.
ISBN 0-9672672-0-X (alk. paper)
1. Lloyd, Benjamin, 1804-1860. Primitive hymns, spiritual songs, and sacred poems. 2. Primitive Baptists Hymns—History and criticism. 3. Hymns, English—Southern States. I. Cauthen, Joyce H., 1944–
BV380B46 1999
264'.064023—dc21

99-36078
CIP

Alabama Folklife Association
c/o The Alabama Center for Traditional Culture
410 North Hull Street
Montgomery, Alabama 36104

PREFACE.

This project was inspired by two sources of wisdom, the great folklorist Archie Green and Elder Donald Smith of Centreville, Alabama. For years, Archie Green has prodded and urged the late Brenda McCallum, Joyce Cauthen, myself, and any other Alabama folklorist who would listen, that we should find and document African American "Dr. Watt's" singers in the Talladega National Forest. Dr. Green was especially interested in the communities recorded by Frederic Ramsey in the 1950s for he suspected they might be using very old tuneless Watts hymnbooks. Joyce Cauthen rose to the occasion, began researching the "Dr. Watts" hymn tradition and found that most African American Primitive Baptists who sing in this style draw their texts from Benjamin Lloyd's *Primitive Hymns*. On a totally separate track, Elder Smith expressed his opinion to me that folklorists and others have not given *The Primitive Hymns* its due. After all, this hymn book, and not the well-studied shape note books, is used in church services. He also pointed out that Lloyd's hymn book represents an older music tradition from which shape note singing developed.

With the financial assistance of the National Endowment for the Arts and the expertise and support of those acknowledged herein, Joyce and I were able to produce for the Alabama Folklife Association this book and compact disc exploring the history of Benjamin Lloyd and his word-only hymn book and presenting a glorious variety of ways in which people sing from it. A theme embedded in all the essays is the persistence of *The Primitive Hymns*. Communities of singers remain devoted to this book, not out of a sense of preservation of a folk tradition, but through a desire to worship God with the assistance of divinely inspired hymns. These churches, associations and individuals scattered across the United States are connected through their shared faith and occasional patronage of The Primitive Hymns Corporation of Rocky Mount, North Carolina. To all who choose to sing praises with the assistance of this hymn book, compiled by a frontier Alabama preacher, we dedicate this work.

Joey Brackner, Director
Alabama Folklife Program
Alabama State Council on the Arts

ACKNOWLEDGEMENTS.

I would like to thank Joey Brackner for conceiving of this project, getting it funded, and asking me to serve as its director. Joey is the instigator of many festivals, publications, recordings, and videos that document Alabama folklife, and it is always a treat to collaborate with him.

All who worked on the project benefited greatly from the involvement of John Bealle. John served as chief consultant, copy editor, index and bibliography compiler, and wrote a splendid introduction to the book. A Sacred Harp singer himself, John shared with us his passion for the subject of hymn singing as well as the objectivity we needed to get our work done and present it well.

I also thank essayists Beverly Patterson, William Dargan and Oliver C. Weaver, Jr., who provided assistance beyond their job descriptions, photographers Anne Kimzey, Aimée Schmidt, Donna Matthews, Susan Roberts, Joey Brackner and Kim Appel who provided us with lasting images of the singers and church buildings; Steve Grauberger, Beverly Patterson, Drew Armstrong and Flawn Williams who provided recordings used on the compact disc, and Philip Foster who mastered them, magically removing the unavoidable sound of air-conditioning from many. I appreciate the artistry and friendship of Bob Weathers of Icon Graphics who designed and published this book and has made many other contributions to the Alabama Folklife Association over the years.

Many people were generous with their time, knowledge, and hospitality. Among them were Bettie Woodard of the Primitive Hymns Corporation, Elizabeth Wells and Becky Strickland of the Samford University Special Collections, Diann Weatherly of the Mervyn H. Sterne Library at the University of Alabama in Birmingham, Don and Regina Clark, Harry Eskew, Bob Gamble, Margaret Anne Kelley, Clarke Lee, David and Kathie Lee, Tollie Lee, Kay Norton, Kevin Nutt, Gaylon Powell, Laurie Sommers, Donald Smith, Alan Brown, Nicholas Temperley, Dan Patterson, Wendell and Virginia Robertson, Jim and Mary Lloyd, Patrick Cather, Eugene and Betty Forbes, Steve Woods, Claude Hand, Edward and Bertha Bell, Fred and Nellie Cockrell, Armond Ritch, Amanda Smith and Ella Pearl White, Hattie J. Allison, James and Martha Collins, Thomas Peterson, Ronnie Houser, Lieutenant Whitfield, Vassie Knott, Ryanna Barnes, Oscar Hardin, Walter Lee, Johnny Ray and Wanda Gardner and Eileen Knott. I especially appreciate the active and unwavering support of Jim Cauthen throughout the project.

Joyce Cauthen

Lloyd's *Primitive Hymns* may be ordered from The Primitive Hymns Corporation, P. O. Box 92, Rocky Mount, North Carolina 27801-0092. Cost is $9.95. North Carolina residents must pay 6% sales tax. Customers will be billed later for postage.

CONTENTS.

Preface v

Acknowledgements vi

Notes on the Authors viii

Introduction 1
John Bealle

Congregational Singing from Benjamin Lloyd's *Primitive Hymns*

I. Hark the Doleful Sound:
The Old Way of Singing in the Original Sipsey River
Primitive Baptist Association 7
Joyce Cauthen

II. Forging Religious Identity:
An Exploration of Hymn Singing in Anglo-American
Primitive Baptist Churches 22
Beverly Patterson

III. Texts from Lloyd's Hymn Book in the Quiltwork
of African American Singing Styles 29
William T. Dargan

Benjamin Lloyd and the History of his Hymn Book

IV. Benjamin Lloyd:
A Pioneer Primitive Baptist in Alabama 48
Oliver C. Weaver, Jr.

V. Elder Benjamin Lloyd and his Hymn Book 57
Joey *Brackner*

VI. The Primitive Hymns:
Descriptions of Extant Editions 77
Compiled by Joey Brackner

Suggested Readings and Recordings 88

Notes to the Compact Disc 90

Index........ 114

NOTES ON THE AUTHORS.

John Bealle served as copy editor, bibliographer and indexer of this publication and consultant to the project director. An independent folklore researcher who has taught at Indiana University, the University of Alabama, and Miami University, he is author of *Public Worship, Private Faith: Sacred Harp and American Folksong* and his work has been published in *Western Folklore* and *Ethnomusicology.*

Joey Brackner is the folklorist for the Alabama State Council on the Arts. As director of the Council's Folklife Program, he manages grants programs which help preserve and present the state's folk traditions. His other research interests include Alabama folk pottery, traditional graveyard decoration and southern horticultural traditions. He is a descendant of both Primitive and Missionary Baptists.

Joyce Cauthen is the author of *With Fiddle and Well-Rosined Bow: Old Time Fiddling in Alabama.* She has served as director of the Alabama Folklife Festival and produced a number of recordings of traditional music, including *Possum Up a Gum Stump: Home, Commercial and Field recordings of Alabama Fiddlers; Jesus Hits Like the Atom Bomb: John Alexander's Sterling Jubilee Singers of Bessemer;* and *In the Spirit: Alabama's Sacred Music Traditions.*

William T. Dargan is professor of music and head of the department at Saint Augustine's College in Raleigh, North Carolina. His writings on gospel singers Willie Mae Ford Smith and C.J. Johnson and his study of congregational singing traditions in South Carolina have been published in the *Black Music Research Journal.* He is currently writing a book on "Dr. Watts" hymn singing.

Beverly Bush Patterson serves as Folklife Specialist for the North Carolina Arts Council where she researches and documents the state's traditional artists and culture and administers a grants program. She consults on a wide variety of public folk arts projects ranging from heritage tourism and museum exhibits to publications and films. In 1995 the University of Illinois Press published her book, *The Sound of the Dove: Singing in Appalachian Primitive Baptist Churches*, and its accompanying cassette of documentary field recordings.

Oliver C. Weaver, Jr., is a descendant of Benjamin Lloyd and a retired Professor of Philosophy from Birmingham-Southern College. For the last thirty years, he has researched and published books and articles about his ancestors. In 1968, he published his article, "Benjamin Lloyd: A Pioneer Primitive Baptist in Alabama" in *The Alabama Review.*

INTRODUCTION.

John Bealle

Benjamin Lloyd's *Primitive Hymns* (1841) is at first glance an unassuming book. The contemporary edition of this nineteenth century hymn book has a simple black cover with gold trim. Its purpose is unquestionable: a massive compilation of hymns for singing—705 hymns on 545 pages, texts closely following one another, often with quatrains separated across pages. Another 31 pages are consumed by indexes—three in all, listing general subjects, particular subjects, and first lines—suggesting the desire for quick access and frequent reference. Besides this there is a two-page preface that has remained unchanged since Elder Lloyd wrote it in 1858. In most every aspect *Primitive Hymns* seems a relic. There is little here to suggest a book of importance.

Yet one fact announces its significance: it is still in print. And with few interruptions and not that many changes it has remained so since its first appearance in 1841. And more than this: while the balance of American religion has undergone repeated transformation and modernization, some congregations still use *Primitive Hymns* in much the same way it was used in the nineteenth century. Clearly, it is not merely a book, but a testament to some diligent and long-enduring custodial attention. It is the story of this love and faith that the authors in this volume are so compelled to recount.

This story concerns not only Lloyd's book, of course, but also the era of the hymn book itself, marked so conspicuously in America by the introduction of the hymnody of Watts and Wesley in the early eighteenth century. From the time of the First Great Awakening, their poetry became a path to greater accessibility and involvement in Protestant worship. As a genre of religious poetry, the hymn transfixed eighteenth century Protestants as a revelation, mapping personal religious experience with frightening clarity. Consequently, in this circumstance of newfound religious freedom, the hymn book stood, alongside the Bible itself, as a vivid map and mirror of the Christian's personal spiritual journey. Elder Lloyd even organized his book as a spiritual chronology, with sections of poems that applied to the journey's various stages.

The hymn book was also a religious instrument that stood at an unprecedented distance from ecclesiastical authority. It was a companion to the lay preacher, who extended salvation far beyond the reach of orthodoxy, and was an essential tool of the frontier circuit rider, who brought religion to areas where Europeans were sparsely settled. By the mid-nineteenth century, however, most denominations had taken at least some centralizing steps. With music, this led to the use of segregated choirs, denominational hymnals, and organs and other musical instruments in worship—devices introduced to atone for the presumed musical shortcomings of congregational singing. It may perplex us, then, that Benjamin Lloyd's hymn book, one of the few to survive this call to progress, appeared precisely at the time its genre was losing ground.

But it does not. As the writers in this volume explain, it was along this very fault line of American Protestantism that *Primitive Hymns* emerged and was assured its tenure. The precipitating issue was the controversy over the mission movement that emerged from the evangelical theology of the Second Great Awakening. Among Baptists, the issue presented itself in debate in associations, the organizational unit that linked small numbers of congregations that shared common beliefs, practices, and resources. Some Baptists objected to missions and other alternatives to worship, and withdrew to form separate anti-mission associations. While most Baptists followed the course of American Protestant modernization, these anti-mission associations, taking the name Primitive Baptist, held fast to the ecclesiastical principles given directly in New Testament scripture. The Primitive Baptist church took its defining stance against precisely those forms of worship which led modernizing denominations into the mainstream of American religious life.

Although the issue of missions was the nominal cause of the split, at root was the nature of authentic Christian worship. Along with choirs, musical instruments, centralized denominational authority, seminaries, and Sunday schools, missions comprised one of the "human inventions" that, Primitive Baptists believed, did not belong in the true church. *Primitive Hymns* thus found its place among those who believed worship music was a direct and unmediated encounter with the Holy Spirit. Those whose testimonies are recorded in this volume bear witness to the power the music sung from Elder Lloyd's book has in their lives.

Surprisingly, very little has been written on Elder Lloyd and *Primitive Hymns* except for a 1968 article by Oliver C. Weaver, reprinted in this volume, that laid out the basic facts of his life. Lloyd was born in 1804 in Hancock County, Georgia, and was baptized into the Baptist church in 1822. In 1832, he was ordained to preach among the churches of the Columbus Association at a time when the course of the anti-mission split was being set. Only the previous year, the Columbus Association had stood their ground against missions, repudiating the Georgia Baptist Convention for its "benevolent enterprises."

In 1834, Lloyd moved to Alabama and began several business enterprises that provided his family prosperity and status. His preaching there was unafflicted by the Baptist division until an anti-mission resolution was adopted and then repealed. In 1838, Lloyd and other anti-mission Baptists withdrew and formed the Beulah Association of the Primitive Baptist Church. It was in the circumstance of this newly formed Primitive Baptist Association that Elder Lloyd was called to duty to provide his church with a hymn book. In 1841, the first edition of *Primitive Hymns* was published. Because Lloyd made provisions in his will for the continued publication of the book, *Primitive Hymns* was kept in print by members of his family with few interruptions until the Primitive Hymns Corporation took over in 1971.

Since Primitive Baptists have no central denominational authority, each congregation adopts the hymn book of its choosing. Through the years other Primitive Baptist singing books were compiled, some with printed music. So today, a variety of books are used among the churches. But Lloyd's has remained in print and has earned much stature among those loyal to the old sound. As these articles illustrate, however, this allegiance is not merely to the book, but to the complex whole of sound and sense that constitutes congregational singing. Even among those congregations or associations who sing from Lloyd's book, there is a wide variety of styles of singing—this variety is vividly apparent in the range of styles on the accompanying CD. Each bears the deep attachment to the sound of the familiar and beloved voices of one's own congregation.

It is the circumstance of this personal attachment to the familiarity of congregational worship that has led some congregations over the years to retain some of the oldest living musical practices of American Protestantism. A few congregations still maintain the practice of "lining-out," whereby a song leader intones a line of text and the congregation repeats this in song. Because hymn books contain no music, singers depend on a small stock of memorized tunes suited to the various forms of poetic meter. Some of these tunes are ancient, having been passed down from memory long before they appeared in printed tunebooks. In the nineteenth century, tunebook compilers transcribed these tunes, set them in three-part or four-part arrangements, and printed these arrangements. Some of the nineteenth century southern tunebooks—notably *The Sacred Harp* (1844) and *Christian Harmony* (1866)—are still used in public singings and are popular among Primitive Baptists who use Lloyd's hymn book in worship services.

In African American congregations, where there is a similar fondness for the "old landmark," Lloyd's hymn book bears additional historical significance. It hearkens to the earliest stirrings of African American Christianity, where hymn singing from the beginning was a fundamental component of worship. This was the time of the First Great Awakening, whose liberating theology provided Christian conversion to many who had theretofore been excluded. The essential themes of this theology were registered vividly by the hymnists—particularly Isaac Watts. Some congregations refer to the style as "Dr. Watts" singing, even though authors are not identified in *Primitive Hymns* nor is Watts the only author.

Perhaps more important than the theology of the text was congregational singing itself, which was saturated with African stylistic traits and performance practices. Hymn singing preserved key elements of African worship, and thus provided a more deeply compelling experience than other aspects of Christianity. In Baptist, Methodist, and Presbyterian slave congregations, hymn books were in great demand, where hymn singing played a central role in conversion. After the Civil War, African Americans formed separate Primitive Baptist associations. Some clung to Lloyd's hymn book and the old sound that went with it.

Primitive Hymns, then, is an important book, one of the few living remnants of the earliest musical culture of America's European settlers, a book linked by the hymns it contains to the earliest development of African American Christianity. But its importance is not as a historical artifact, but rather as a testament to long-enduring faith. It is this story the authors in this volume seek to tell. Their focus is on the role of Lloyd's book in contemporary worship and on its extraordinary perseverance as a hymn book.

In "Hark the Doleful Sound: The Old Way of Singing in the Original Sipsey River Primitive Baptist Association," Joyce Cauthen focuses on a single Primitive Baptist association, the Sipsey River Association, originally organized around African American churches in the Sipsey River area of west Alabama. It was founded in 1872, at a time when African American Primitive Baptist churches were forming separate associations. At first linked geographically to the river, its range has changed with doctrinal differences, population shifts, and ease of travel. Today the association consists of eighteen congregations, two of them in Detroit, Michigan. They have a devout allegiance to the "Dr. Watts" style of singing and still have song leaders able to line out the hymns. Cauthen retraces the roots of the "old way of singing," its introduction into African American Christianity, and its development in Primitive Baptist associations in Alabama.

In "Forging Religious Identity: An Exploration of Hymn Singing in Anglo-American Primitive Baptist Churches," Beverly Bush Patterson focuses on the unique sound of congregational singing, so dear to those who sing from Lloyd's book. Through compelling testimony, Patterson illustrates the connections between congregational singing and the everyday lives of church members. Religious traditions, many preserved over centuries, are among the most deliberate aspects of Primitive Baptist life. Yet, while there is an overall consistency to Primitive Baptist theological and aesthetic principles, actual practices are widely varied among congregations and deeply personal for church members themselves. Consequently, with Primitive Baptist music, one finds profound attachment to the sound of one's own congregation and considerable variation in the styles of singing in different churches. This variation in style is vividly apparent on the CD. It is at the juncture of personal and congregational experience that religious identity is forged. Thus Primitive Baptist music, Patterson maintains, concerns not merely aesthetics, but the whole of the spiritual experience from which the compelling loyalty to this book derives.

William T. Dargan, in "Texts from Lloyd's Hymn Book in the Quiltwork of African American Singing Styles," examines African elements of performance practice in African American congregational singing from *Primitive Hymns*. Turning aside the question of origins that mired previous scholars, Dargan examines the significance of the "style synthesis"—whereby English hymns were wedded with African music and worship practice—that occurred between 1750 and 1850. In resolving essential cultural differences, hymn singing supplied a key condition for the extraordinary spread of African American Christianity during this period. As Dargan illustrates with analysis and detailed transcriptions, this synthesis survives in contemporary hymn singing where each song provides unique stylistic reference—in elements of rhythm, melody, and performance practice—to cultural self and other. From the earliest slave conversions to contemporary "Dr. Watts" Primitive Baptist singing, African American hymn singing has been a compelling form of worship as well as a paradigmatic act of American diversity.

"Elder Benjamin Lloyd and his 'Hymn Book'" is Joey Brackner's account of the publishing history of *Primitive Hymns*. Brackner begins, of course, with the idea of the hymn book itself, recounting the extraordinary impact of Watts and the movement of the dialectic of orthodoxy during the eighteenth century. A century later, with the rise of the Primitive Baptists, the hymn book found itself set deliberately against a backdrop of religious modernism. This was the circumstance of *Primitive Hymns*, a book compiled by Elder Lloyd for his church out of a sense of duty, having perceived that "no one of the Primitive denomination had stepped forward" to provide a hymn book for the anti-mission churches. Over the course of four years after it appeared, he made significant changes to the book and then in 1845 produced the third edition, which with few exceptions established the content of the book for its entire history. Brackner surveys this history, examining Lloyd and his family on the nineteenth century frontier, the various publication arrangements, the sources of the hymns, and the relation of Lloyd's book to other hymn books. In "*The Primitive Hymns*: Descriptions of Extant Editions," a complement to his study of Lloyd, Brackner examines each edition chronologically, noting the changes made and the reasons for them. In compiling this record of the unrelenting attention Primitive Baptists have given *Primitive Hymns*, Brackner takes account of the deep love they have for this book.

These authors bring long-overdue attention to Lloyd's book, recounting its unusual historical depth and cultural breadth. But, wisely, they look beyond Lloyd's book to the extraordinary people who have loved it and cared for it for a century and a half. It is this story of perseverance—of a hymn book that has inspired the most steadfast reverence for singing hymns to God—that brings to bear the brief moment of historical awakening that is this collection of articles.

HARK THE DOLEFUL SOUND:
THE OLD WAY OF SINGING IN THE ORIGINAL SIPSEY RIVER PRIMITIVE BAPTIST ASSOCIATION

JOYCE CAUTHEN

A certain kind of singing in African American churches astounds visitors. George Pullen Jackson first heard it as a youth in a Southside church in Birmingham, Alabama. Later, as an adult musicologist, he tried "to make melodic sense out of what still seemed musical chaos." In *White and Negro Spirituals* (1943), he described the music and the uninitiated listener's reaction to it:

> A deacon or the elder "lines out" a couplet of the text in a sing-song voice and at a fair speaking pace ending on a definite tone. This "tones" the tune. The deacon then starts singing, and by the time he has sung through the elaborately ornamented first syllable the whole congregation has joined in on the second syllable with a volume of florid sound which ebbs and flows slowly, powerfully and at times majestically in successive surges until the lined-out words have been sung. Without pause the deacon sing-songs the next couplet and the second half of the four-line tune is sung in the same manner. ...It seems perfectly simple and easy for the singers. But the listening white person is utterly confused, cannot make musical head or tail out of what he hears. His concepts of melody, rhythm, music, fail to help him through the maze. He cannot even check the trend by the words he has heard lined out; for the singing surges on with so many graces and strings of graces (entwined about longer notes which he feels must be parts of an unfolding melody), that all words, syllables even, lose their identity and evade recognition.[1]

Jackson called hymns sung in this manner "surge songs," a term of his own invention which has never found favor among scholars or singers. Others use the terms "meter music" and "old one-hundreds" for such hymns. The congregations that Jackson visited called them "Dr. Watts hymns," a term widely used in the South and one which we shall use throughout this essay. It was derived by transforming the name of the revered English hymnist Isaac Watts into an adjective that denotes a particular way—the "old way"—of singing hymns. Actually, many texts sung in this style were written by others. None of the four "Dr. Watts" hymns on the accompanying CD (*Primitive Hymns* #241, #440, #364, #3) came from the pen of Isaac Watts.

The words to "Dr. Watts" hymns are drawn from text-only hymnals such as Benjamin Lloyd's *Primitive Hymns*, and the tunes are drawn from memory. While many selections in text-only hymn books, such as "Amazing Grace" and "Blessed Be the Tie that Binds," can also be found in those with musical notation, it would be totally unacceptable for the leader to use a tune drawn from a music book in a context in which a "Dr. Watts" hymn is expected. He would instead use one of a small stock of tunes that has been retained in the congregation's memory over many generations.

From what are these tunes remembered? Where did these slow, meandering tunes, so unlike those sung in most churches today, originate? When one hears them sung in an African American congregation, it is difficult to believe that they came from anywhere except Africa. Though he later learned differently, George Pullen Jackson noted that on first hearing them he thought he was "listening to a perfectly preserved hangover of African folk ways. The singing seemed so completely exotic."[2] Instead what he heard was a musical form derived from the earliest experience of African American Christianity, a complex blending of African musical practice and the "old way" of English psalm singing brought to New England in the seventeenth century.

English Roots of the Old Way of Singing

The congregational singing style of the New England colonies had developed in England after psalm singing was introduced in 1559.[3] Texts from the Book of Psalms were rearranged to fit the meter of popular folk tunes, so that worshipers could easily sing them, and meter markings, such as C.M. (common meter), L. M. (long meter), and S.M. (short meter) were placed above each psalm to indicate which tunes would fit that text. When first introduced, the psalms may have been sung in lively fashion, for their detractors called them "Geneva Jigs." After a few generations sang them without organ accompaniment or musical direction they were more like dirges than jigs. Nicholas Temperley explains that they diverged from their folksong roots because folksongs were usually accompanied by dancing, clapping, and other bodily movements as well as fiddles and lutes. In church, where such accompaniment was considered inappropriate, "people had to sing the tunes without assistance; the less confident singers no doubt waited for the leaders to move on to the next note, and then followed them after a time lag; and so a natural 'drag' developed that imperceptibly slowed the normal speed of singing as years went by." There is no doubt, says Temperley, that the Pilgrims and Puritans would have been familiar with this very slow style before they left the English shores.[4]

Slow tempos may also have been the result of lining out, a practice sanctioned in 1644 by the Westminster Assembly of Divines. This body issued *A Directory for the Publique Worship of God Throughout the Three Kingdomes of England, Scotland, and Ireland* which instructed that "for the present, where many in the Congregation cannot read, it is convenient that the Minister, or some other fit person appointed by him and the other Ruling Officers, do reade the Psalme, line by line, before the singing thereof."[5] Writing of customs in churches of New England in 1726, Cotton Mather said, "In some [churches], the assembly being furnished with Psalm books, they sing without stop of reading between every line. But ordinarily the Psalm is read line after line, by him whom the pastor desires to do that service; and the people generally sing in such grave tunes, as are the most usual in the churches of our nation."[6]

Other characteristics of New England psalmody have been recorded for us in the writings of a group of educated clergymen who detested most congregational singing of the early 1700s. For instance, Rev. Thomas Walter spoke of the "various Twistings of the old Way, and that too according to the *Genius* of most of the congregations."[7] Reverend Thomas Symmes felt that the psalm tunes were corrupted in being "handed down by *Tradition* only" and disliked the "many *turnings* or *Flourishings with* the voice."[8] "Jeoffrey Chanticleer" (probably James Franklin) wrote of the gradual lowering of the pitch while singing a psalm, saying that the congregation would fall from "a cheerful pitch to a downright *Grumbling.*" To be able to continue singing, individuals would raise their voices to sing at intervals of a fourth, a fifth, or an octave above the pitch of the song leader.[9]

When the negative bias of the reformer's descriptions is removed, we learn from such statements that psalm singing was a traditional art, preserved in memory rather than written notes, in which tunes and style varied from congregation to congregation. The tunes were rendered in highly ornamented fashion and were not sung in unison, as singers added parts to suit their voices. They were lined out and sung very slowly. We can easily see the resemblance between this form of singing and the "Dr. Watts" hymns that astonished George Pullen Jackson.

Reformers called for improvements in congregational singing that could be brought about with musical training. In England during the eighteenth century, organs were installed in large Anglican churches, stringed instruments were used in smaller ones, "religious societies" endeavored to improve their singing, and choirs were formed.[10] By the close of the century, these approaches had been successful in advancing the "regular way" of singing in the new nation. And, writes Temperley, "after the second Great Awakening of around 1800, revival hymnody of various kinds swept through the Middle Atlantic, Southern, and Western states, and with the aid of shape note tunebooks, there was a vast extension of the ability to sing from notes. Entirely new tune repertories replaced the old metrical psalm tunes and even penetrated the conservative rural churches that resisted all attempts at reform of singing practice."[11]

During this period of conflict between those who would sing in the old and regular ways, a hymn book arrived in the colonies that was embraced by singers on both sides of the issue. Before Watts's *Hymns and Spiritual Songs* was published in England, congregations sang only rewordings, many of them poetically awkward, of the Psalms. Watts objected not only to the strict metrical psalmody of these compositions, but also to the fact that their subject matter did not encompass the New Testament. His original compositions were meant to correct that situation. Though some believers objected that the new hymns were man-made concoctions that should not replace the word of God as expressed in the Psalms, many others embraced and imitated them, contributing to "the flood of hymn writing that has caused the eighteenth century to be looked upon as the 'Golden Age of English Hymnody'."[12] According to David W. Music, "the purposeful simplicity and attention to practical detail of Watts's poems commended them to persons of all ages and educational levels, while their evangelical flavor made them excellent vehicles to accompany preaching in the Puritan and Independent churches of the day."[13] Watts knew that his hymns would be lined out, even though he preferred that they not be. In his introduction to the 1793 edition of *Hymns and Spiritual Songs* he explained that "the unhappy mixture of reading and singing . . . cannot presently be reformed."[14] For this reason he continued the practice of writing in meters which provided natural stopping places at the ends of lines, thus accommodating those who sang in the old way.

The Introduction and Survival of the Old Way of Singing in African American Worship

It was in the eighteenth century, while the old and regular ways of singing coexisted, that large numbers of Africans and African Americans were evangelized and converted to Christianity. Following the success of George Whitefield, revival preachers like Shubal Stearns (Baptist) and Samuel Davies (Presbyterian) brought hymn singing, Biblical narrative, and the theology of personal salvation to slave congregations in the middle and southern colonies.[15] As Davies noted in letters to John Wesley, slave worshipers were "exceedingly delighted with Watt's Songs," and he sought more hymnals and materials for use in religious instruction. When books and hymnals arrived, Davies wrote:

> All the books were very acceptable, but none more so, than the Psalms and Hymns, which enabled them to gratify their peculiar taste for psalmody. Sundry of them lodged all night in my kitchen; and sometimes when I have awaked at two or three in the morning, a torrent of sacred psalmody has poured into my chamber.[16]

In Davies' phrase "torrent of sacred psalmody" lies the suggestion that the converts were singing in the old way, a style still called "Dr. Watts" by African Americans who sing it.

During this period of religious revival, the Great Awakening, Davies and other "New Light" evangelists converted thirty-one thousand slaves to Baptist and Methodist sects, using Watts' hymns sung in the old way as a conversion tool.[17] Thus, while the old-way of singing was on its way out elsewhere, thousands of African Americans in the South were embracing it for the first time.

The next wave of revivalism to sweep the country at the beginning of the nineteenth century inspired other forms of sacred music that some congregations sing in addition to "Dr. Watts" hymns. This Second Great Awakening penetrated further into the slave states of Kentucky, Tennessee, and Alabama, fueled by spirited camp meetings. Kentucky became the center for such meetings, with three thousand blacks and whites attending the first such revival at Cane Ridge (1801).[18] Camp meetings provided an atmosphere of unprecedented cultural synthesis not only because they allowed and encouraged free religious expression, but also because they bore some similarity to African religious practice.[19]

Preaching, praying, and singing were at the heart of these multi-day, pan-denominational gatherings. Song leaders drew hymns with simple texts and images from special camp meeting songsters and set them to easy tunes, allowing everyone to participate in the music.[20] Also leaders sang more complicated texts by Watts, Wesley, and others, then encouraged the worshipers to join in with a simple repetitive chorus of camp-ground composition, such as "I'm bound for the promised land, I'm bound for the promised land, Oh who will come and go with me, I'm bound for the promised land." Some of these choruses became refrains that were attached to any number of hymns and were later transcribed in works like Ira Sankey and Dwight Moody's *Sacred Songs and Solos with Standard Hymns,* which enjoyed widespread popularity among black and white singers.[21] Today there are African American congregations, such as the Spring Hill Union Association of southeast Alabama, that sing common, short, and long meter hymns in "Dr. Watts" style as well as hymns in meters such as "8s and 11s" and "P.M." with added choruses that became popular at camp meetings.

In 1822 Charles Colcock Jones and Charles Cotesworth Pinckney spearheaded a movement with the goal of getting planters to Christianize their slaves. They sought to convince planters that religion would make slaves more obedient. Furthermore, if planters showed interest in their slaves' souls this would lend justification to the institution of slavery. They succeeded in persuading many slave owners to build "praise houses" led by itinerant white Baptist, Methodist, and Presbyterian preachers and supervised by overseers or members of the planter's family.[22] On plantations where slave gatherings were forbidden or where the slaves failed to find religious fulfillment in services provided, African Americans organized secret or "invisible" churches. Here they sang spirituals—sacred songs of their own making that had special meaning in the context of slavery. Here also they gradually transformed Anglo-American psalmody, learned from missionaries and preserved in memory, into a distinctive Afro-American form of hymn singing which retained vocal traits from their African heritage.[23]

After Emancipation, when independent black churches were being organized throughout the South, "Dr. Watts" hymns became more deeply entrenched in African American worship while spirituals lost favor among some of the congregations. Wyatt Tee Walker considered the attraction of the metered music:

> First of all, the quatrain form, or four-line form, of the Watts-style hymn lent itself to easy rote memory during a period when illiteracy was widespread. Following the war, as literacy increased, the quatrain, like the Bible, was a natural and easily available practice ground for the new skill. Secondly, as physical structures developed, formal worship services, as distinct from the religious meetings of the praise houses held on the plantations, began to supplant the earlier forms of worship associated with the "invisible church." The "new" hymns fitted this "new" arrangement. The day of open-end religious meetings had passed with the end of slavery. Thirdly, and just as important as the other two, an expanding religious consciousness—influenced by the new conditions of the social context—gave to the ex-slaves a sense of a larger religious identity beyond the slave consciousness forced upon

> them for so long. Now they were free and would sing the music of the larger community about them as an assertion that they took seriously their belonging.[24]

Though the hymns were hardly "new" at the time perhaps Walker is referring to the fact that the growing literacy allowed them to add many more hymns to their repertoires and gave new impetus to singing the metered music.

Eventually, however, the practice of singing in the "Dr. Watts" style began to wane. In the twentieth century, as black churches acquired musical instruments, as more worshipers gained musical education, and as gospel music was accepted into worship services, many churches stopped singing in the old way. But just as there were those who would not stop singing spirituals because of their association with slavery, there were those who would not allow the "Dr. Watts" hymn to die. Churches with members who wished to embrace the newer music and members who revered the old hymns and felt them unsurpassed in their spirituality made arrangements acceptable to both. The old singing style was retained in deacon-led devotionals held before regular morning services in which more contemporary sacred music predominated. Thus today "Dr. Watts" hymns are still sung in the devotionals of mainstream urban churches with large congregations as well as in small rural churches.

The tradition is somewhat diminished in churches with two "frames" of worship, as Walter Pitts calls them, for in the first frame they typically sing only one hymn, such as "A Charge to Keep I Have" or sing a number of hymns to the same tune.[25] However, there are clusters of churches whose doctrines are highly compatible with "Dr. Watts" singing. These conservative churches, which do not sanction musical instruments or choirs, sing primarily in the old way and have retained more tunes. We shall now examine one of those clusters, the Original Sipsey River Association of the Primitive Baptist Church, to see how and why this centuries-old form of singing survives today.

Singing in the Sipsey River Association

The Sipsey River Association celebrated its 125th Anniversary on August 31, 1997. According to Association historian Sister Nellie Cockrell, it was organized in 1872 with the assistance of white Primitive Baptists of the Old School Primitive Baptist Association.[26] Bethlehem Primitive Baptist of Eutaw, founded in 1850, became the mother church of the Sipsey River Association, which consisted of twenty-nine African American churches of West Alabama and Eastern Mississippi. Many of these churches were formed after the Civil War, some by African Americans who had previously attended Anglo-American Primitive Baptist churches. As happened elsewhere in the South, the white association members may have helped organize the new association rather than have individual black congregations seek affiliation with them. They may have provided information on conducting annual meetings and on taking and publishing minutes, and they may have provided models for the Sipsey River Association's articles of faith and rules of decorum. If the individual churches that became part of the association were not already using Lloyd's *Primitive Hymns* as their hymn book, they probably would have been introduced to it at this time. However, the style in which they sang the hymns was not influenced by the white Primitive Baptists. They continued to sing in the style their ancestors had learned long ago and made their own, a style they shared with other black Baptists and Methodists.

The Sipsey River Association was centered near the junction of the Sipsey and Tombigbee Rivers, though there were also congregations to the east in Tuscaloosa and Jefferson Counties. Over the years doctrinal differences, geography, and other factors caused some congregations to leave the Association and others to join it. For instance, the Mississippi congregations are no longer affiliated, but two congregations in Detroit, founded by Alabamians relocating there in the 1930s, are members of the Association. The Association now consists of eighteen congregations in Greene, Pickens, Tuscaloosa, and Jefferson Counties, Alabama, and in Detroit, Michigan. Today it is Interstate 59/20 which links the Alabama churches of the Association rather than the Sipsey River. Between Bessemer and the Mississippi State line, none are far from that river of traffic.

The congregations range in size from 100 to 6. In general, they are composed of older people, retired from working as farmers, teacher's aids, health and domestic workers, etc. Many have helped their children through college and into middle-class professional lives, often in distant cities. Young and middle-aged people stand out in Sipsey River congregations because there are so few of them.

Each Alabama congregation meets only once a month, while the Detroit churches meet weekly. When their own church is not in session, members fill the pews of other Sipsey churches, thus congregations with only a few active members and no deacons will have fifteen to twenty people and a number of borrowed deacons at a regular service and many more at the semi-annual footwashing services. Association members know each other and the customs of associated congregations almost as well as they do their own. They also have an opportunity to worship together at three-day Association meetings three times during the year. These meetings are attended by members of the Detroit churches as well as associations that correspond with the Sipsey Association, predominantly from Tennessee and Georgia. All Sipsey congregations and other associations they correspond with, regardless of their geographical locations, sing from Lloyd's *Primitive Hymns*.

The church buildings of the Sipsey River Association are small and well-kept. Constructed of wood, brick or concrete block, they usually consist of a sanctuary with a lunchroom behind it and a vestibule flanked by two restrooms in front. There are no stained glass windows or any kind of decoration except for one large painting or wall hanging of a Biblical theme and photographs of elders, past and present. Though plain, the churches are not Spartan, and usually have padded pews, air-conditioning and heating, and a small public-address system. Most have concrete baptismal pools outside.

While conceding to some creature comforts, the Sipsey River Association struggles to remain true to the ways of the early Christian churches. Their congregations do not have Sunday school classes, instrumental music, choirs, usher boards, women's and youth fellowships, nor any of the other activities by which other churches attract new members and allow them to participate in the services. Women are not allowed to lead hymns, testify, or vote on church matters. Though all members are aware that such practices discourage young people from attending church and cause membership to decline as older members die and are not replaced, they are uncomfortable with change, especially changes incompatible with church doctrine. As Primitive Baptists, they believe in predestination. "We believe," states one of the Articles of Faith, "in the doctrine of election by grace and that God chose His people in Christ before the foundation of the World." "We believe," says another, "that God's elect shall be called, converted, regenerated, and sanctified by the Holy Spirit."[27] Because God selects his own and reveals their salvation to them personally, there is no reason for the church to reach out to others through Sunday schools, revivals, and other programs. God's elect will find the church themselves. Once they have, it is the church's business to provide them a gathering place for worship, renewal, and enlightenment, and the opportunity to participate in the ordinances of the gospel—"baptism and the Lord's Supper, and the washing of the saints' feet."[28]

One does not go to a Sipsey River church to make business connections, to be seen in one's best clothes, to hear musical performances, to talk politics, or to be educated on any subject other than scripture. One goes in search of an intense worship experience. Metered hymns sung in the old way are crucial in creating and sustaining the spiritual intensity of the service.

At about 10:30 on a Sunday morning, deacons will cut short their conversations and move to their places at the front of the church. The women chatting in their pews stop and direct their attention to a deacon standing at the front. Holding the only copy of Benjamin Lloyd's *Primitive Hymns* in the sanctuary, he opens the prayer service or devotional with a few words of welcome, then calls out the number and first line of a hymn. Immediately the congregation starts singing, moving through the lines one slow, embroidered syllable at a time. Each syllable gets four long beats, thus a word like "amazing" takes twelve beats to sing. When the congregation reaches the last word of the second line, the deacon intones the next two lines at a quick pace, half speaking, half singing them. This alternation of quick lining out and slow singing goes on until the deacon has sung as many verses as desired. At the close of the first hymn, he is likely to say that the first hymn is to clear our hearts and voices or to put us all in accord. Then he will raise a second one or pass the hymnal to another deacon to do so.

The congregation has been sitting through the first hymn and the first verse of the second. But as the deacon lines out the beginning of the second verse, all rise to their feet and move to a place where they take into each hand the hand of another worshiper. In clusters and lines that reach across pews and aisles, they rotate their joined hands in time with the music. As they sing each syllable, they make three rotations and close the syllable with a strong pulse on the fourth beat. They shake hands with two people throughout a four-line verse, then move to another place in the hall and fellowship with two others. During the last verse they make their way back to their seats, only to rise from them again when other hymns are sung during the service.

Ceremonial handshaking, called "fellowshipping" in the Sipsey River Association, is practiced in a variety of forms in black and white Primitive Baptist congregations across the nation. The form and frequency with which it is done in the Sipsey River Association has much to do with the way the hymns are sung there. For instance, the slow, steady foot pounding that

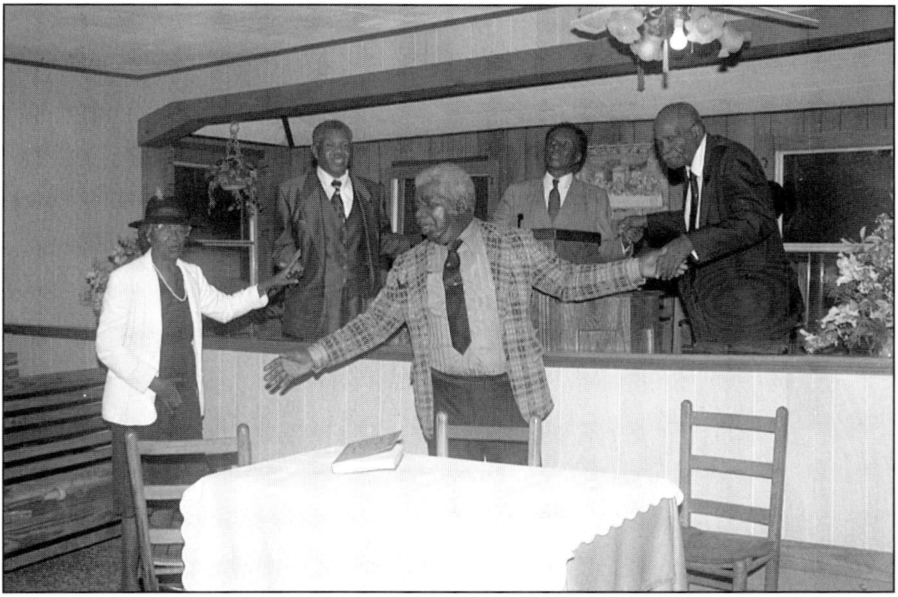

Aimée Schmidt

Fellowshipping at New Hope Primitive Baptist Church, Eutaw, Alabama, 1994

underlies the singing in other black Primitive Baptists churches is not heard here, nor, for obvious reasons, is hand clapping. Instead the strong, muscular rotation of the arms provides rhythm and lets singers know when to release one syllable and begin the next. It imposes form on what might be formlessness and prevents the drag that Temperley identified as inherent in the old way of singing.

The handshake also makes lining out a necessity. With their hands involved in fellowshipping, singers cannot hold a hymnal and thus depend for the words on the hymn raiser or on memory. If the deacon or elder delivers the text unclearly, the congregation will be reduced to humming. If he skips a line or mispronounces a word, the congregation will do so as well. Unless the hymn is very familiar, it is likely that words will be mumbled, anyway. At such a slow pace of singing, it is very easy to forget the complex and archaic words before it is time to sing them. In this context, it may be that the words are not as important as the reverential mood created by the singing and the creation of a community of worshipers through the joining of voices. The manner in which the hymn raiser calls out the words definitely influences the spirit in which they are sung, however. On hymn #364 of the accompanying CD, for instance, the passion with which Elder Frank Eatman calls out the last two lines of the second verse raises the intensity of the singing to a higher level.

At the close of the second hymn, a long prayer by a deacon, knees on the floor, head bowed into the seat of his chair, may elicit "moans" from individuals in the congregation. This term refers to improvised singing from the congregation. Someone—male or female— will feel inspired to sing out a phrase such as "He's been good to me," "Down here waiting on you," or "You've been a doctor to me." Others in the congregation may join in and sing it two more times, at a tempo and pitch similar to those of "Dr. Watts" hymns. The moans may go on for awhile before a deacon softly raises another hymn. The formal text will suddenly rise amidst the colloquial phrasing of the moans, and voices will come together in the third hymn of the service, (as heard prior to hymn #364 on the accompanying CD). Another prayer and hymn or two follow and the intensity of the service builds until the spiritual excitement is palpable throughout the sanctuary.

At this point an Elder steps up to the pulpit, signaling the end of the Devotional. In many churches, including the more progressive Primitive Baptist congregations that have left the Sipsey Association, a choir will enter with the Elder and a pianist or organist will set the tempo of all music that follows. This, according to Walter F. Pitts, Jr., is the second part of a two-frame service, which Pitts sees as a holdover from African ritual. In *Old Ship of Zion: The Afro-Baptist Ritual in the African Diaspora,* Pitts observed that in the first frame, the slow, lined out Euro-American hymns are sung to prepare the congregation for the "descent of the spirit," which will take place in the second frame to more upbeat, modern music of African American origin. In the Missionary Baptist churches in Texas that Pitts served as pianist, no one was ever possessed by the spirit during the Devotional. If one were inspired to "shout," he would stifle it until the appropriate time in the second frame. Similarly, the old style "Dr. Watts" hymns would never appear in the second frame, unless set to instrumental music played in a way to lead to trance.[29] In the Sipsey River Association, however, old-style hymns are sung throughout and the Holy Spirit is as likely to possess a worshiper during the first hymn or prayer as during the last.

After the service is placed in the hands of the elder, scriptures are read, sermons preached, and collections are taken up. There are no printed programs and the order and length of the service varies from congregation to congregation. In addition to a sermon by the elder, there are likely to be scripture readings and sermons by any of a number of visiting elders and licensed ministers. Each may ask the congregation to sing a particular hymn prior to his sermon. A hymn is also sung when the church opens its doors to any who wish to join and at the close of the service. All hymns are sung in the old way.

The Sipsey River Association mainly sings texts that are identified in the hymn book as short, long, and common meter—the meters of most hymns sung in the seventeenth and early eighteenth centuries. To "Dr. Watts" hymn singers, these meter markings have nothing to do with number of beats per line or rhythm. They simply indicate which tune to use with a particular text. The tune most commonly sung in the association can be heard on the accompanying CD as hymn #440. Whenever anyone raises a short-meter hymn, such as "Blessed be the tie that binds" (#196) or "Beside the gospel pool" (#161), he will use this tune. I attended a Sipsey River church service in which six out of seven hymns were sung to it. Mt. Hebrew of the Spring Hill Union, on the other side of the state from the Sipsey churches also sings "Beside the gospel pool" to this tune though at a faster pace.

Sister Nellie Cockrell refers to the tune of a hymn as "the rise and fall of it." After listening to the rises and falls or the contours of sixty hymns recorded at Sipsey services, I have come to the conclusion that there may be only four or five tunes sung in the Association. Singers who regard subtle differences in the embellishments on a basic tune as a reason to consider it an entirely different tune may feel there are many more. George Pullen Jackson and many others who have tried to analyze and transcribe "Dr. Watts" hymns have indicated that it is very difficult to distill the basic melody out of the embellishments enough to identify a tune with confidence. However, William Dargan made excellent transcriptions of the four hymns in that style which are included on the accompanying CD. Were more hymns so clearly transcribed, we could better identify the Sipsey Association's tunes and use this information in comparative studies of others who sing in this style.

The only music other than "Dr. Watts" hymns heard during a Sipsey service is in the form of spirituals. Spirituals can be initiated by anyone in the congregation prior to the service or while offerings are being collected. In the morning service three separate collections are taken, one for the minister, one for the church, and one for the poor. Each paper bill and coin is counted and recounted in view of the congregation, and a financial report is given. During this lengthy process, talented singers will lead venerable spirituals like "In that Land" or "Standing in the Need of Prayer" or they may introduce ones they have recently heard, like "I've got a Good Mind to Count them Angels." Because the spirituals are in call-and-response form, the congregation easily joins in the singing, sometimes clapping their hands and swaying to the music. There is controversy among members about the appropriateness of spirituals in the service, however, and some Sipsey congregations do not sing them.

The Sipsey River Association strives to hold to the "old landmark," their term for the doctrines and practices of the association when it was founded in 1872. The way it conducts communion and footwashing services exemplifies this desire. Held twice a year, in May and September, these pageant-like services draw many observers as well as family members returning to the church from far away. During a short break at the close of the morning service, the women of the church, who have dressed in white for the occasion, cover their heads in simple cotton kerchiefs and put white aprons over their clothing. The men of the church prepare the communion table, bring in the pitchers, basins, and stacks of linens needed for washing feet and rearrange the pews so that one faces another. A deacon raises one hymn to bring everyone into order for the service, then hymn #240, "Twas on that dark and doleful night," and a prayer follow. Amidst the moaning and shouting which the prayer inspires, elders and deacons gather around a table at the front of the sanctuary to pour homemade wine and break unleavened bread which has been prayerfully baked by the church Mother. An elder reads Biblical passages of the Lord's Supper, others expound upon the scripture, and a deacon raises hymn #241, "That doleful night before his death." After partaking of the sacraments at the table, deacons pass them out to the congregation, warning that only those who have examined themselves and are right in their souls should take communion. Layers of sound fill the sanctuary—the elders' chant-like exegesis of scripture, the singing of moans like "I'm just sitting here trying to hold my peace" or "Something just keeps on bothering me," and the shouting of those filled with the Holy Spirit.

When all have partaken and the communion set is removed, elders begin to read and discourse upon passages from the thirteenth chapter of John, in which Christ washes his disciples feet and dries them with a towel around his waist. As one reads and preaches, another wraps a long unbleached domestic towel around his waist and follows Christ's example. Deacons pour water from battered metal pitchers into large enamel bowls and place them in the aisles beside each pair of facing pews. Elders and deacons wash one another's feet at the front of the sanctuary while the churchwomen participate in the ceremony at their seats. The women nearest the aisle in each set of pews wrap the long towels around their waists, bend to wash the feet of the women they are facing, then dry their feet with the end of the cloth. When the other has reciprocated, they stand and embrace each other, then pass the linens and basins to those seated beside them. A third hymn, #258, "Did Christ the great example lead," is sung as the footwashing continues. At its conclusion the congregation without prompting begins hymn #49, "Hark the voice of love and mercy." This hymn, being in the particular meter, is a departure from all others they sing. Though it is lined out and sung slowly, the syllables are not held out the customary four beats, but are rendered as quarter and eighth notes. The last couplet of each verse begins with the phrase "It is finished," and these two lines are repeated giving the effect of a chorus. But the congregation soon returns to the old way of singing when, after words from an elder or a prayer, they sing #196, "Blessed be the tie that binds," to the customary short meter tune.

It is a long, complex service with many details of language, action, music, and dress that have been preserved solely by memory and practice through the Association's long history. In an association that strives to adhere to the old landmark in this way, it is easy to understand how the old way of singing has survived.

But will it continue to survive? Given the advanced ages of the members and the inability of the Association to attract more than a few young people, this question is never far from the minds of Sipsey leaders. The Association may hold its own in size because people tend to be attracted to its serious spirituality as older adults. But these converts will not have grown up singing in the old way. And even those who have grown up as Primitive Baptists were not raised, as the older members were, in homes where family and neighbors gathered regularly to sing from Lloyd's *Primitive Hymns* during the week. The singing of "Dr. Watts" hymns seems destined to "stop by degree," a phrase Deacon Edward Bell of Mt. Pilgrim uses to describe the gradual decline in the quality of metered hymn singing. He and other senior members mourn the passing of the days when "those old folks could really sing."[30] However, the late Deacon James Collins felt that the old way will endure. When one feels God's call, he or she gains the ability to sing the hymns, or at least the ability to learn them with effort. With the help of the congregation and the use of a tape recorder, said Collins, new members can learn to sing in the old way.[31]

The Old Way of Singing in a New Century

Our nation's earliest form of Christian music still survives. Small numbers of Amish, Old-Order Mennonites, Old Regular Baptists of Kentucky, Crawfordite Primitive Baptists of South Georgia, and Creek Indians in Oklahoma continue to sing in the slow, ornamented style of the New England colonies.[32] And large numbers of African Americans whose ancestors learned and cherished "Dr. Watts" in the early eighteenth century still sing in that

Donna Matthews

Footwashing service at Bethlehem Primitive Baptist, Eutaw, Alabama, 1996

style today in churches across the nation. Some sing only a few hymns in the old way. Others, like the churches of the Sipsey River Association, sing only in the old style. In such churches, be they African American, Euro-American or Native American, the old way of singing identifies them as conservative believers who cherish the worship traditions of their elders. Their hymns are effective in creating and sustaining the degree of spiritual intensity they desire in worship services and they have no desire to adapt more modern forms. In such churches members sing with great vitality and skill, insuring the survival of the old way well into another century.

Notes

[1]George Pullen Jackson, *White and Negro Spirituals: Their Life Span and Kinship* (New York: J.J. Augustin, 1943), 248-49.

[2]Jackson, 249.

[3]Nicholas Temperley, "The Old Way of Singing: Its Origins and Development," *Journal of American Musicological Society* 34 (1981): 516.

[4]Temperley, 523.

[5]Quoted by Temperley, 532.

[6]Gilbert Chase, *America's Music: From the Pilgrims to the Present*, revised 3[d] ed. (New York: McGraw-Hill, 1987), 21.

[7]Chase, 26.

[8]Chase, 28.

[9]Chase, 33.

[10]Temperley, 536.

[11]Temperley, 536.

[12]David W. Music, "Isaac Watts in America Before 1729," *The Hymn* 50 (January 1999): 29.

[13]Music, 29.

[14]Isaac Watts, *Hymns and Spiritual Songs* (London: J. Bruce et al., 1793), viii.

[15]Lillian E. Easton-Ashcraft, "African American Christians During the Colonial Era," in *Encyclopedia of African American Religions*, ed. Larry G. Murphy, J. Gordon Melton, and Gary L. Ward (New York: Garland, 1993), 198.

[16]Dena J. Epstein, *Sinful Tunes and Spirituals: Black Folk Music to the Civil War* (Chicago: University of Illinois Press, 1981), 104.

[17]Walter F. Pitts, *Old Ship of Zion: The Afro-Baptist Ritual in the African Diaspora* (New York: Oxford University Press, 1993), 77.

[18]Pitts, 46.

[19]Portia K. Maultsby, "Music in the African American Church," in *Encyclopedia of African American Religions*, ed. Larry G. Murphy, J. Gordon Melton, and Gary L. Ward (New York: Garland, 1993), 521.

[20]John Bealle, *Public Worship, Private Faith: Sacred Harp and American Folksong* (Athens: University of Georgia Press, 1997), 36.

[21]Pitts, 77-82.

[22]Pitts, 51-53.

[23]Chase, 69.

[24]Wyatt Tee Walker, *"Somebody's Calling My Name": Black Sacred Music and Social Change* (Valley Forge: Judson Press, 1979), 90.

[25]Pitts, 150.

[26]From notes by Sister Nellie Cockrell in souvenir program of 125th Anniversary Program of Sipsey River Association, August 31, 1997.

[27]Abstract or Articles of Faith, *Minutes of the 123rd Annual Session of the Sipsey River Primitive Baptist Association Number One,* 1995, 51.

[28]Ibid.

[29]Pitts, 149-153.

[30]Edward Bell, interview with the author, Mt. Pilgrim Primitive Baptist Church Livingston, Alabama, January 25, 1999.

[31]James Collins, interview with the author, Tuscaloosa, Alabama, January 1, 1997.

[32]On Creek Indian hymn singing, see Willie Smyth, *Songs of Indian Territory*, (Oklahoma City: Center of the American Indian, 1988). Smyth writes that Creek hymn singing, which has much in common with the "Dr. Watts" tradition, began in the southeastern United States long before the Trail of Tears.

FORGING RELIGIOUS IDENTITY:

An Exploration of Hymn Singing in Anglo-American Primitive Baptist Churches

Beverly Bush Patterson

People with a love for American spiritual songs have long recognized Primitive Baptists as conservators of one of the oldest and most powerful traditions of American religious folksong. But even in the Southern Appalachians and parts of the lowland South and middle Atlantic states where they were a strong presence only a century ago, Primitive Baptists themselves are little known and barely visible to outsiders. On the surface, they blend easily with their neighbors. Their homes are typical of others in areas where they live, and so are their occupations. A congregation in southwestern Virginia, for example, includes former textile mill and furniture factory workers, a retired highway construction worker, a nurse, a public school teacher, a cafeteria worker, an insurance salesman, a beautician, a downtown merchant, a secretary, homemakers, and farmers.

In their churches, however, Primitive Baptists distinguish themselves, keeping beliefs and practices that have not changed substantially for more than two hundred years. Some congregations still gather at the river to sing and baptize those who have asked for "a home in the church." They practice an old way of unaccompanied, congregational hymn singing that is an outgrowth of seventeenth-century psalmody in the British Isles and the American colonies and of early eighteenth-century hymnody. Their unyielding adherence to the "hard" predestinarian doctrines of particular election and salvation by grace, combined with old-time practices such as footwashing, dinner on the ground, and monthly worship services, have increasingly set them apart from mainstream churches, from their more evangelical neighbors, and from most other Baptists. In addition, they have insistently upheld principles of congregational autonomy and resisted forming any national organization. Their preservation of these older traditions has encouraged their critics to view them unsympathetically, and often simplistically, as "backward," as the last vestiges of a religious subculture that flourished in the Upland South in the late-eighteenth through the nineteenth centuries.

One of the first Primitive Baptists I met challenged this stereotyped view. A retired farmer and stonemason, he recognized other stonemasons by their work and delighted in pointing out the distinguishing characteristics of their work and of his own. He was a fiddle player whose tastes ran to the country music and old-time stringband music that was popular locally. He was also a highly regarded Primitive Baptist preacher, a great singer, and one of the chief song leaders in the churches he served. He had learned to read shape-note music notation in singing schools when he was a young man, and had even helped teach the singing school. Over the years, he had also exercised gifts as a poet and songwriter. Although he was fond of traditional dance and ballad tunes, he especially loved the old hymns.

He was also a student of church history, knowing well that the churches he served had deep roots in Europe and England. Their most immediate predecessors were the seventeenth-century English Particular Baptists—Calvinistic Baptists who underwent their chief development after being transplanted in America. Like most Primitive Baptists, he traced the lineage of the churches he served to the Welsh Tract church, which became a member of the Philadelphia Baptist Association in 1707.

These predestinarian Baptists took the name "Primitive" Baptist around 1830 when a group of their churches withdrew fellowship from the Baptist majority that had begun to embrace Arminian practices (implying salvation through works). The Primitive Baptists rejected the Sunday schools, missionaries, missionary societies, seminaries, and numerous other forms of outreach and development that their more evangelical-minded brethren had adopted. They considered such things "human inventions." According to their Calvinistic interpretation of the Bible, God had already chosen those who would be saved, and any human efforts to save sinners were not only ineffective but were misguided and presumptuous as well. Their adversaries called them "anti-mission" Baptists and "hardshells," and attacked them as backward and ignorant. They, however, called themselves the "Old School" or "Primitive" or just the "Old" Baptists to emphasize their identification with the early New Testament church.

Their architecture, like their singing, reveals the consistency of a set of aesthetic principles that has held fast over almost two centuries. Typically, the newer churches remain very plain—one room—usually without steeples or

Anne Kimzey

Primitive Baptist churches, such as Little Hope Primitive Baptist in Eoline, Alabama, are typically plain—one room—usually without steeples or stained glass windows, even when congregations can afford them.

stained glass windows, even when congregations can afford them. Some of the oldest churches have two front doors, separate entrances for men and women, who once sat separately. Only a few congregations continue to practice separate seating in the congregation, but men and women still have their own "amen corners"—the members' pews that flank both sides of the pulpit. This architecture is consistent with members' views of their church as a refuge and resting place, a home for others like themselves who describe their experience of the world as that of pilgrims and strangers. It is also consistent with their social organization which gives men and women well defined roles: men take the public roles as preaching elders and church spokespersons; and women exercise great influence in maintaining the fellowship within their own local congregation as well as among their sister churches.

In their religious lives, then, Primitive Baptists appear to be deliberately maintaining traditions, many of them orally transmitted, established by their predecessors in the period of the early republic. Why, in the absence of any church authority, do they continue to do this? What kinds of cultural meanings might be embedded in these preferences? My interest in exploring such questions has focused on one of the most distinctive practices in Anglo-American Primitive Baptist churches: their hymn singing.

Unlike most denominations, Primitive Baptists do most of their hymn singing before the service even officially begins. Unwary visitors who ask what time the service begins and then appear at that time often find themselves arriving later than anyone else. It is customary in these congregations for members to gather in the church half an hour or more before the time scheduled for preaching. They sit down and sing hymns together, taking each request in turn, for at least thirty minutes, sometimes longer.

Even non-musicians notice several distinctive things about this singing. Most obvious is that no musical instruments are accompanying the singing. Musical instruments are not even present. Primitive Baptists claim biblical authority for unaccompanied singing and they do not allow musical instruments in the church.

Almost as obvious as the absence of musical instruments is the fairly slow and often irregular rhythm of the hymn singing. Individual congregations have established their own ways of singing the old hymns. Their song style, free and powerfully emotive, is largely dictated by oral traditions, and commonly varies in tempo from one congregation and association to another. As anyone who tries to keep a steady beat by tapping a finger quickly discovers, a regular beat is rarely present. This, of course, is in dramatic contrast to music these same singers enjoy—and may perform—outside of church.

The singing in church is not only unaccompanied, it is also congregational. While solo singing and individual instrumental performances are common outside the church and in other denominations, musical performances by choirs, soloists, or other special groups have no place in Primitive Baptist worship. The exception is the occasional lining-out of a hymn. In this practice—a form of responsorial singing established in the 1640s for congregations that had few books or members who could read—the song leader chants a line or two of the hymn and the congregation responds, singing the same text to the hymn tune. Sometimes the singing is in unison. Sometimes singers improvise harmonies that reflect the influence of other religious music, especially gospel songs and shape-note hymn books.

Although Primitive Baptist hymn and tunebooks have been available since the late-nineteenth century, many congregations continue to use Benjamin Lloyd's *The Primitive Hymns* (1841) or D. H. Goble's *The Primitive Baptist Hymn Book* (1887), which contain only texts. As a consequence, they must sing all of their tunes by memory, and they draw on long-standing oral traditions for hymn tunes that are often as distinctive as the manner of singing. Even when congregations choose a favorite hymn like "Amazing Grace," for example, they may opt for a melody other than the familiar "New Britain" tune. While some of their tunes are widely known and sung in many Protestant churches, others derive from folksongs and do not appear in any tunebooks used by Primitive Baptists or other denominations. Some of these are based on minor-sounding melodies that have what some singers call an old "lonesome" sound. Still others are reminiscent of long-forgotten eighteenth-century psalm and hymn tunes.

A sampling of hymn texts reveals yet other distinctive characteristics that mark Primitive Baptists. In particular, these texts rarely express much assurance of salvation. Unlike Southern Baptists, Primitive Baptists do not sing hymns like "Blessed Assurance, Jesus is Mine." Their theology and their experience embraces too much doubt and uncertainty to claim assurance. They claim, instead, a "hope" of salvation, an experience described in lines like the following from an Old Baptist hymn by an unknown author:

> Mixtures of joy and sorrow I daily do pass through;
> Sometimes I'm in a valley, And sinking down with woe.
> Sometimes I am exalted, On eagles' wings I fly;
> I rise above my troubles, And hope to reach the sky.
> (*The Primitive Hymns,* #384)

Also absent from their repertory are songs like "Wayfaring Stranger" that mention a reunion of families in heaven. Primitive Baptists do not believe that recognition of family members and friends from this life will be a part of their soul's experience in heaven. Occasionally, songs that Primitive Baptists have in common with Methodists and other Baptists show small but telling differences in the texts. In *The Primitive Hymns*, for example, a chorus attached to the hymn "O land of rest for thee I sigh" (#689) begins "We'll wait till Jesus comes." This text is more consistent with Primitive Baptist belief than "We'll work till Jesus comes," which appears as both title and chorus in hymn books of other denominations.

As outsiders, then, we might describe Primitive Baptist hymn singing in general as an old style of unaccompanied congregational singing that draws heavily on oral tradition for its tunes and selects texts that express its predestinarian doctrine and experience. If we were to look more closely at this singing in its historical, musical, and theological contexts, we might gain a fairly comprehensive view of the tradition. We might even assume that our understanding would correspond to that of most Primitive Baptists.

The fieldwork and interviews that are the basis for the discussion that follows proved that was not the case, however. When Primitive Baptists themselves talked about their hymn singing, they referred to the sound itself. Often I heard a casual and passing reference to the "joyful sound," but a few church members went into more detail. One preacher recalled a story he had heard about a soldier from North Carolina who was in a foxhole—maybe in Korea. The preacher said:

> And [the soldier] started singing "Jesus lover of my soul." And as he sang it the enemy came upon him. And the one verse, I believe it's the second verse, speaks of protecting even his head. And when he sang that, the enemy approached him. And they embraced each other. And they separated, and went on their way, both ways.

His comment on the story was this: "I find it a very moving story…that [even enemies] can detect the sound, which is what it's all about.… It all falls back to the sound." The preacher said that he believed children of God had experiences like this and that such experiences show that church membership is not the test of whether or not one is a child of God.

This did not mean the church was not important. He was emphatic about that. A deacon joined this conversation with a reference to the dove, a one of their favorite representations of the church. The deacon pointed out two things about doves: first, that "they build the sorriest nest you've ever seen," and second, that they would not have anything to do with other birds. The preacher made a third point about doves that referred directly to singing. "Well, another thing too about the dove," he said, "is the sound that the dove carries. There's no other bird—even a mockingbird cannot mock the sound of a dove. And that's the reason so many apply the representation of the dove to the church, is that the church has that sound which nobody else can [have]."

My interpretation of these and other similar comments is that Primitive Baptists recognize in the sound of their singing a complex religious identity. That is, they hear a certain sound as representative of the Primitive Baptists. More than that, however, they interpret that sound as evidence of being a child of grace, and they further interpret the sound as a representation of the "true church" which they believe transcends time and place, race and creed.

On the basis of such comments, one might think that the singing in all Primitive Baptist churches would sound very much alike, at least to Primitive Baptists. But, as the accompanying recording demonstrates, even though congregations hold in common a preference for unaccompanied singing and may themselves use the same hymn book, their singing can be quite distinctive. Primitive Baptists themselves said they heard substantial differences in congregational singing among their churches. A visiting preacher's wife confirmed this in a church where her husband often preached when she leaned over toward me during the singing one evening and whispered, "I just can't sing with these people." She told me after the service that I would find that the singing varied greatly from church to church, even among those using the same hymn book. And she supposed that all Primitive Baptists thought the singing in their own home church was the best.

I had been struck by the variety of hymn books used by Primitive Baptists and by the wide range of publication dates, from 1841 to 1983. In addition to Benjamin Lloyd's *The Primitive Hymns* (1841) and Goble's *The Primitive Baptist Hymn Book*, which were favorites with many churches, I found some churches using a third nineteenth-century publication, *The Hymn and Tune*

Book (1886) compiled by Elders Silas H. Durand and P. G. Lester. This latter book offered tunes harmonized in four parts along with the texts. Later publications with both texts and tunes also had a following. These include Elder C. H. Cayce's *The Good Old Songs* (1913), Elder John R. Daily's *Primitive Baptist Hymn and Tune Book* (1918), and various editions of the *Old School Hymnal* (Monsees 1963; and Green 1964, 1983).

Although it seemed only natural that some differences in singing could flow from using different books, the differences were far too great to be solely attributable to that. Some congregations clearly had a taste for the old minor-sounding tunes and liked to have them lined out occasionally. Others preferred the more cheerful sounding major tunes and would rarely, if ever, sing the old minor or modal melodies. Many congregations had abandoned the old practice of lining out years ago. Typically, song leaders were men, but sometimes women filled this role.

Differences in singing were often subtle—tempos moved slightly faster in some churches than others. Some song leaders pitched the songs high, some pitched them low. Sometimes the tunes themselves were different. One elder, when asked how a certain tune went, said "different ways in different places," and then sang the version he liked best. His response was consistent with Primitive Baptist practice. Church members who are unyielding in their insistence on being in accord about fine points of doctrine will notice and accept numerous differences in singing as they visit their sister churches.

Some differences in singing would naturally result from the use of different hymn books and the leadership of different song leaders. The "given" that all this diversity of hymn books presupposes is, of course, congregational autonomy, a basic principle that all these churches inherit from the congregational wing of the British Reformation. No national committee or denominational publishing house usurps the congregation's own decisions in the matter of music.

What, then, does influence the choice of hymn books? We might imagine that the diversity might derive from one of the stereotypical traits of the Primitive Baptists, such as their extreme sensitivity to doctrinal subtleties—that they would reject a hymn book because of certain texts it held. This, however, does not appear to affect their choice. Although some Primitive Baptists find Arminian sentiments in a few of the 705 hymns Benjamin Lloyd compiled in *The Primitive Hymns*, the hymn book remains popular in their churches. All these churches simply expect any compilation of human composure to be flawed. They therefore pick and choose among the texts in any hymn book they use, avoiding texts, or parts of texts, they see as unsound.

Modernization and the degree of economic development in the neighborhoods of the churches and in the lives of members of the various congregations have also failed to correlate with hymn book choices. Some rural churches use newer books than churches in the largest towns in the region. Random factors such as contacts between a song leader and the compiler of a hymn book, or simply the personal taste of an influential elder or song leader plays a greater role. The use of two books—those of Elder Cayce and Elder Monsees—is probably due to the fact that these elders had traveled through a particular region preaching and left behind an affectionate regard for themselves and their books.

What is true of hymn books is probably true also of tune repertories of the churches: that is, that song leaders and elders have had considerable influence upon the shape of each church's song tradition. The musical scores printed in some of the hymn books do not control the congregations' choice of tunes. Few people in any congregation read the notes. A song leader simply lifts a tune, and the rest follow that lead. The tune may be the same as one printed for that hymn, be completely different, or be only somewhat different. I have sung with congregations that easily follow the song leader in substituting completely different choruses for those published. It is not uncommon for them to add choruses where none exist in their hymn books.

Random happenstance, then—the travels and personal contacts of a songbook compiler, or the musical taste of a song leader—may help give a distinctive shape to the song tradition of each local church. But this again is only a partial explanation of the diversity in singing among these churches. One song leader complained that although he loved minor tunes, felt them to be the best suited for meditative texts, and tried to use them in three churches he was invited to pastor, some congregations would not sing them. Whenever he began one of the old minor tunes, he said, the congregation would sing poorly or would turn silent.

The best hypothesis for explaining both the similarities and differences in Primitive Baptist singing—the one that best correlates with outsider observations and members' comments—is that underlying the choices a congregation makes about singing is an impulse to assert a distinct local identity. Even within the limits of a religious song tradition that excludes musical instruments, choirs, and special performances, it is still possible for a group to exploit a range of variations not only with hymn books and repertory, but also with melody, rhythm, harmony, and even tempo and pitch. And that is exactly what these churches do. Although members recognize a general Primitive Baptist "sound," their own specific religious identity is even more rooted in the particular sound of their own home church.

This fact, made apparent in interviews and observations, is not incidental but key to a central impulse in this denomination. Primitive Baptists place great importance on being in fellowship with their home church, normally the church where they actually joined and were baptized. I hear occasionally about persons who for various reasons have been excluded from the church. One deacon said, "If you get out here and…carry on like the world does, the first thing [Old Baptists] do, they bring you before the church. And if you're not willing to quit that and repent from that, somebody'll make a movement and a second to exclude you and you're on the outside." In Primitive Baptist practice, if you are put out of your home church, you may be "out" of that whole community. No other Primitive Baptist church in that fellowship network will knowingly admit you to the privileges of membership. As the deacon put it, "You've lost your voice."

The distinctiveness of the Primitive Baptist song tradition, and the differences that appear within it, do not reveal themselves in the written historical record. Neither do they imply a passive following of tradition or just the random happenstance that one might assume from the Primitive Baptist heritage of congregational autonomy. Their musical differences are, instead, the distinguishing sounds of a particular spiritual home.

TEXTS FROM LLOYD'S HYMN BOOK IN THE QUILTWORK OF AFRICAN AMERICAN SINGING STYLES

William T. Dargan

As patterned differences invoke an aesthetic tension in quilts, so do regional hymn-singing styles among black Baptists form a tapestry of diverse means converging upon similar ends. The tensions accrue from the relative influence of African and English approaches to singing as well as from the social change that came with early colonial life—the growth of slavery as an institution, the national period, the religious awakenings, Emancipation, Post-Reconstruction, and black urban migration. These sacred performances can be pathos-filled or celebratory, sharply percussive or intricately melodic, awash in archaic harmonies or guided by a solitary melody. The eight performances of texts from Lloyd's *Primitive Hymns* featured in this offering—all, save two, recorded in Alabama—reflect the style synthesis that occurred between 1750, when the Great Awakening revivals were well afoot, and 1850, by which time the outdoor camp meetings, Baptist missions to slaves, and shape note singing had made a composite impact upon American Protestant tradition.[1] Save the missions to slave quarters which came later, all these developments were in progress well before Alabama attained statehood in 1817.

The colonial eighteenth century had witnessed an exponential growth in the enslaved African population to meet the demand for labor to farm tobacco and rice in the planter colonies of Maryland, Virginia, and Carolina. The exigencies of these growing slave communities melded with the religious moment in a series of revivals during the 1730s and 1740s, and small but significant numbers of slaves were converted in the prolonged period of religious fervor that became known as the First Great Awakening. These were the earliest stirrings of black hymnody.

Stemming from such efforts, the first black Baptist congregation was organized in Virginia in 1758, and according to Mechal Sobel, by 1800 at least ten more had been organized in Virginia, the Carolinas, and Georgia.[2] Here and there, slave quarters were aflame with revival. The Calvinist evangelical ministers were phenomenally successful wherever they preached. However, their access to slave plantations was limited to places where only a few slave owners—many of them recent converts—were beginning to allow missionaries access to their human property. The Christian gospel was not preached to the majority of slaves until long after the American Revolution.

As cotton supplanted tobacco and rice as the major export in the early 1800s, the Louisiana Territory was purchased, and the land economy sustained by slave labor expanded westward. During this period, black congregations would multiply and the migratory growth would move from Virginia

Susan Roberts

Deacon Willie B. High of Mt. Pilgrim Primitive Baptist, Livingston, Alabama

through the mountains into Kentucky and Ohio, and across the Delta regions of Alabama, Mississippi, and Louisiana, into Arkansas, Texas, and Oklahoma. Sobel notes the establishment, following the founding of the African Church of Mobile in 1806, of six other black Baptist churches in Alabama by 1850. As the byproduct of such migratory sifting, the imprint of African and English as well as oral and written influences began to bring forth an intricate pattern of regional styles among black worshippers in the former slave-holding states.

Not surprisingly, the chief dynamic of this cultural sifting was a creative tension between black-to-white and white-to-black transfers. Such transfers occurred between various oral traditions, including German, Scotch, Irish, and likely African as well. The historical picture of this creative tension was clouded, however, by the abundance of early nineteenth century printed tunebooks by white compilers that included tunes common in both black and white oral tradition. For scholars such as George Pullen Jackson, these printed sources suggested a predominantly white origin for this shared tradition. In fact, many of the tunes published in the early 1800s come to us *through* rather than *from* written sources. It is unfortunate that reliance upon written transcriptions led Jackson to conclude that only white-to-black transfers had occurred.[3] For at the time he outlined his theory in *White and Negro Spirituals* (1943), some of the former slaves whose words are documented in the slave narratives could have sung what hymns they remembered from oral traditions.[4] Even then the extent of African contribution would have been difficult to measure. However, from the present distance, it would be impossible to retroactively estimate the influence of slave oral traditions upon the plethora of tunebooks published between 1800 and 1850.

Working from what can be known, #263, "What wondrous love is this," appears as typical of the kind of traceable adaptation that tunes published in written sources (e.g., "Wondrous Love," *The Sacred Harp*, p. 159) seem to have undergone within black congregations. The rhythmic lilt of "Wondrous Love" is retained and elaborated through repetition, and a more spare and iterative melody is substituted which lends emphasis to the rhythm. The gorgeously contoured melody is, as it were, flattened out. To the untrained ear, this might seem to take away what cannot be replaced. The majority of the pitches in the duet by Amanda Smith and Ella Pearl White hover around two notes, the home pitch of the key and the third above it. But this narrowed melodic range causes the ear to hearken to any note rising above or falling below these two as being of special importance. This is the economy of up-and-down idiomatic expressions, question and answer musical phrases that drives the chant-like intonation of African American spirituals, as well as sermons and prayers. While its melodic development is less traceable, #270, "O May I worthy prove to see," also sounds like a tunebook melody that may have been reworked so as to conform to the speech rhythmic character of an African American vocal tradition.

More apparently African sounding and less melodically familiar, other performances included here bear less immediate resemblance to published tunes. Exemplary of this greater cultural distancing is the relationship between #440 and the tune "Idumea" (e.g., *The Sacred Harp*, p. 47).[5] Although the melodic detail of #440 stands in sharp contrast to "Idumea," the larger melodic contours are almost identical: a first line begins and ends on the tonic or home note; the second leaves and returns to the fifth; the third moves from the fifth back to the tonic; and the fourth, like the first, hovers about the tonic. While this larger similarity is undeniable, there is something no less significant about the sequence of smaller melodies that is strung together from the melismas that color every syllable of #440. Although the rhythm is freely measured, there is a sense of pulse connected more to the flow of the words as breath phrases than to any sense of metrical regularity. While the printed version in *The Sacred Harp* pushes the ear toward the sound of the whole, the sequence of self-contained embellishments in the recorded performance of #440 beckons the ear and the consciousness to savor the very moment of each syllable. These stylized melismas are heard in a far more predictable rhythmic context in #3, "Amazing Grace." In her transcription, Ruth Crawford Seeger diligently notates every rhythmic idiosyncrasy.[6] Whereas she described in detail the musical phenomena that *resulted* from certain procedures, I have sought in the transcriptions here to prescribe how the melody might be practically *replicated* (or at least seen as a series of formulaic rhythmic motives). A third group of tunes performed by black congregations (see #364 and #695) are either from oral (perhaps African) sources, or they have been so thoroughly transformed and adapted to African American style principles as to make their written source(s) unidentifiable.

Whether the melodic sources are clear, questionable, or unknown, one can observe a conceptual unity within diverse examples of black Primitive Baptist hymn singing. This claim of a distinctive musical and ritual style among African Americans has been most fully substantiated in works by Eileen Southern (1997) and Dena Epstein (1977), who have noted the problems already cited in Jackson's argument for the white origins of black spirituals.[7] The polemical and sustained debate during the first half of this century over black and white origins of the spirituals revealed the inherent weakness of either claim as an extreme. More recent scholars have seen as self-evident the relative and mutual influence of African and English musicality upon blacks and whites in America. Such a broadening of perspective is reflected in studies like *America's Musical Landscape* by Richard Crawford and *The Power of Black Music* by Samuel Floyd.[8] These works rightly mediate without ignoring the debate as to whether the spiritual's origins were white or black, and assume the continuing interrelationship between these factors as a defining feature of America's inherent diversity.

Nevertheless earlier writings by Jackson (of Vanderbilt University) and by John W. Work III (of Fisk University) remain especially important to the study of hymn singing among Primitive Baptists. We are indebted to Jackson for his extensive inventory of hymn tunes among whites, and to Work for the prescience of his insight in recognizing the distinctive nature of hymn singing among blacks. In a 1949 article on "Changing Patterns in Negro Folk Songs," Work wrote that, while another author

> . . . deplores the passing of the spiritual, . . . I personally grieve much more over the passing of this "Dr. Watts." There is something epic, something elemental, something overwhelmingly religious about the rendition of these old songs. Starting softly and informally, as one of them does after the half-intoned wordphrase by the leader, a melody is spun-out melismatically

> with no rhythm derived out of measure and beat, only punctuated by the wordphrase of the leader. The crescendo is gradual but relentless, and at a high point in the song the membership rises and engages in a very dignified formal clasping of hands between members right and left. Sometimes the singers, particularly the deacons, circulate among the membership. There is nothing trite, banal, or sensational in this performance.
>
> There seems to be no musical descendant of this grand old song type. Certainly no art form has embraced it or derived anything from it. The great American composer, R. Nathaniel Dett, attempted to incorporate something of this long meter in "Chariot Jubilee," one of his most ambitious choral works. There is a melismatic flavor characterizing the singing style of Negro folk music today which may very well be derived from these earlier 'Dr. Watts'."[9]

Three of the West Alabama performances (#241, #440, and #364) are especially illustrative of Work's perception of "melody spun-out melismatically with no rhythm derived out of measure and beat." By contrast, #695—one of two non-Alabama performances included here—*is* sung in a rhythm apparently "derived out of measure and beat." Yet, paradoxically, I will argue that the comparison between them may reveal more similarity than difference. Of the eight selections performed by black congregations, the style and practice of these four is most undeniably African. While the other four performances (#3, #263, #270, and #382) employ some of the same practices, the overall contours if not the details of the latter melodies are more readily identifiable with the Anglo-American tunebook tradition of shape note singing, such as that of *The Sacred Harp*. Because such written sources codified Anglo-American, and by implication, African oral traditions as well, the distinction between written and oral "sources" is best understood as one of degree rather than nature. Most significantly, written transmission facilitated wider patterns of regional and national dissemination.

The conceptual framework that obtains in all these cases and makes African American song style distinctive is what linguist Geneva Smitherman has described as speech rhythms or "songified speech."[10] This way of speaking and singing is a mode of ritual performance that derives from the widespread distribution of tonal languages in the West and Central regions of Africa from which slaves were taken. In such cultures, the lexical meanings of words are still determined by the relative placement of their syllables in a vertical system of high, medium, or low pitches. The English language makes no allowance for such a system of meaning. But African American speakers and singers have evolved an approach to performance—whether in standard English or various regional dialects—which manipulates the expressive potentials of language and music in ways that are analogous to the concept of African tonal languages.

Enslaved Africans also brought with them a tradition of circle dances out of which the African American ring shout tradition developed. But the religious context they embraced from the colonial period onward was also musically grounded in the iambic prosody of hymnists like Watts, Wesley, John

Newton, and Horatius Bonar. This English language imprint was centered in the jog-trot or rhythmic flow of iambic prosody, most often in either common meter (four lines, including 8, 6, 8, and 6 syllables), long meter (8, 8, 8, and 8), or short meter (6, 6, 8, and 6). Popular hymn texts, such as "Amazing grace, how sweet the sound" (common meter), were often sung as verses to these songs, which were popularized as "spirituals," and the slaves (and white worshippers as well) developed other formulaic couplets following similar patterns. For example, this familiar "wandering chorus" is a blended trope of the 8-7-8-7 pattern known as particular meter and the 8-6-8-6 common meter:

> If you cannot preach like Peter (8 syllables)
> If you cannot pray like Paul (7)
> You can tell the love of Jesus (8)
> And say he died for all (6)

In a more African way, certain word phrases and chantlike melodic formulas were utilized to constitute the chorus of repetitively insistent songs like "Jesus is a rock in a weary land," "Go down, Moses," or "I got a home in that rock." These "mascons," or mass concentrations of meaning, mark points of reference in sermons and sayings which carry force by way of allusion. An example of such an approach to sound and words is heard in #695, a shout-like performance that gains momentum throughout its course. Though the text is strophic instead of repetitive, the percussive quality of the melody suggests chant, and the tension between strictly measured singing and freely measured lining out lends intensity to this extended performance. Not only is the chant-like melody itself sung by the full congregation, but as the performance develops, the full congregation also chants or lines out the words intermittently in unison along with the leader. Much more than a mere redundancy, this practice signifies the primacy of lining out as a worship moment from which the rhetorical gestures of black musicality have proceeded. The chant generates rhythmic momentum by working against the prevailing beat pattern to frame an inhalation or tension-producing moment, wherein a speech-like diction proceeds in unmeasured rhythm. Then in the percussive measured rhythms that quickly follow, that same energy finds release.

Speech rhythms surface in musical contexts that are either freely measured or strictly measured. Traceable to the practice of moaning,[11] freely measured speech rhythms are the most speech-like in character and most often occur in the slowest hymn singing styles. Strictly measured hymns that are lyrical (e.g., #263) contain poignant but understated rhythms, and most clearly betray the influence of Anglo-American folk sources. Strictly measured hymns that are percussive (e.g., #695) gradually accelerate throughout the performance and often culminate in the holy dance or shouting episodes.[12] Freely measured (irregular) speech rhythms can be heard, for example, in #241, where the hymn leader lines out the words in more or less definite pitches, but with rhythms owing more to speech than to song. Somewhat measured (regular) speech rhythms are more noticeable in the melody that follows. However, this hymn, as a whole, as well as #440 and #364, are in a style which emphasizes freely more than strictly measured speech rhythms. The freely measured character of chant that opens most lining out hymns is based upon the movement that Pitts has documented in black ritual from standard English to regional dialects as the worship fervor intensifies.[13]

The musical implications of freely measured speech rhythms may be heard as either "portraiture sound" or "poetic rhythms." Both derive from the kind of moaning tradition which Willie Collins has investigated in Southeast Alabama churches.[14] Preceding #364, an example of such a moan issues from the improvised phrase, "Wanna feel your Holy Spirit."

While portraiture sound stretches and pulls notes in ways that suggest contortion or distortion (irregularity), poetic rhythms utilize formulaic (regular) successions of notes to form the melismas (three or more notes sung to one syllable) noted above by John Work. Portraiture sound consists of slides between notes, hollers, growls, and other gestures which expand the range of sound colors and textures comprising a single performance. In #241, many of the phrases intoned by the leader and by the congregation are remarkable for the slurred or liquid sound of movement from one note to the next. Also included in this complex are the subtle changes of color that lend emphasis or nuance to any given melodic gesture. Poetic rhythms, such as those of the leader in #241, utilize two or three-note rhythmic-melodic cells as a stimulus to the rhythmic and melodic momentum of the performance. The frequency of use and expressive range of a certain poetic rhythm determine whether it will strike the ear either as a well-worn cliché or as just that measure of familiarity which enables *and* inspires the congregation to follow the unspoken musical directions of a gifted leader. For example, although no "new" material whatsoever is heard in the leader's singing of #241, the timing, range of vocal colors, and judicious reference to formulaic melismas bring about a sustained growth of intensity in the singing.

As freely measured speech rhythms are divisible into portraiture sound and poetic rhythms, so are strictly measured speech rhythms either percussive or lyrical. Strictly measured rhythms that are lyrical strike a balance between the "spirit" or expressive freedom of unmeasured chant and the "letter" or constraint of a discernible, if changing pulse. Of the four categories of stylistic devices—poetic rhythm, portraiture sound (both unmeasured), and percussive speech rhythms (measured) being the other three—lyrically measured speech is the closest to the melodic ideals of Anglo-American folk tradition. While such melodies bear resemblance to Anglo-American models, their melodic movement is narrowed or flattened, suggesting a more sharply defined sequence of repetitive rhythmic phrases. In this way, measured speech rhythms (whether percussive or lyrical) can ascribe a chant-like insistence which implicitly associates the melody itself with the character of the time lines or ostinato rhythmic patterns that can be heard in many African musical traditions. An example of speech rhythms that are percussive is heard in #695, which uses the words throughout to mark an accelerating rhythmic pattern. Performed by the Shiloh Primitive Baptist Association, which includes churches from North Carolina, Virginia, and Kentucky, such percussive speech rhythms mark a regional singing style which holds wide currency among Primitive and Missionary Baptists Associations in the Piedmont Region of the Carolinas that surrounds Charlotte, North Carolina. Whereas this uplands shout style is founded upon offbeat syncopated rhythms, the more African ring shout of Low Country and sea island areas builds upon cross-rhythmic clapping and stomping patterns. The orthodoxy of Primitive Baptist faith has established almost no presence in the latter areas where the influence of African language and culture has been most persistent.

Epstein has documented the early presence of African musical instruments and performance styles in the New World and historian Sterling Stuckey has argued that sacred dances such as the ring shout attended secret worship among African slaves from the seventeenth century onward.[15] These factors suggest a larger context wherein enslaved Africans modified the worship forms committed to them by white Baptist and Methodist missionaries. In this process, the linguistic influence of hymn singing became an incubator wherein Anglo-American forms were adapted to African principles of musical and ritual organization. For example, the Afro-Baptist devotional developed as a modification of white Baptist forms, alternating between sung and spoken worship. Building upon this model, a complex of vocal gestures such as moaning and hymn singing became prominent in black Baptist devotionals, and the repetitive rhythms of black preaching culminated in the celebratory postures of shouting. This conforms to Pitts's findings on the African origins of the structure of black Baptist worship and suggests that the devotional was Africanized and the shout Christianized by blacks in North America during and after the Great Awakening of the early nineteenth century.

The quiltwork of black regional hymn-singing styles was homespun in North America from the imported yarn of both African musical structures and Anglo-American melodies and texts between 1750 and 1900. Although significant numbers of blacks and whites in Virginia and the Carolinas were introduced to the hymns by Whitefield and Wesley in the 1740s, 1750 is offered as a beginning point because journal entries from the 1750s by the Revs. Samuel Davies, Hutson, Todd, and Wright suggest that the slaves were singing these hymns in a way that was noteworthy if not distinctive by that time.[16] These gleanings note the zeal among slaves for learning to read the scriptures and their gift for singing the hymn texts. No less important to the development of black hymn singing styles was the African correlation between singing and movement. The Rev. John Watson's 1819 warning against what he called "Methodist error," became the earliest detailed description of the African-derived ring shout, a religious circle dance accompanied by cross-rhythmic clapping and call-and-response singing.[17] As European-derived hymn singing among slaves predated Watson's 1819 description by seventy years, it is also evident that the African-derived musical practices he described had been in evidence even longer.

Therefore, as the slaves memorized the hymn texts, the given Anglo-American melodies were revised to suit variously African musical structures and ritual patterns. In this course, the texts of Watts and Wesley remained at the center of a developing African American regional style complex which would later subvert the Protestant orthodoxy of hymn texts to surreptitious pleas for deliverance from the injustices of slavery. This subversion came not so much in outright protest, but in texts that spoke to the existential problems of suffering and death with which slaves were familiar. For example, black folk hymn couplets, sometimes attached to Anglo-American hymn texts as choruses, emerged during slavery or in the dark night of violence and intimidation of the post-Reconstruction era.

My work on earth will soon be done (8)
And then I'm going home (6)

Another frequently heard couplet was this:

I'm not too mean to serve the Lord (8)
He's done so much for me (6)

Following emancipation, the texts of Watts and Wesley remained vital sources of hope to the differing sensibilities of increasingly separate congregations of white farmers and former slaves who had worshipped jointly during the antebellum period. But by the year 1900 several developments were brought to bear on the rural farm economies that encompassed and nourished lining out and other facets of the old-time religion. For example, the institution of Southern sharecropping extended the ethos of slave culture, the hopelessness of freedom without empowerment began to wreak havoc on the souls of black folk; and the self-help of either black vocational (by Booker T. Washington) or liberal arts education (by W. E. B. DuBois) was being touted as the next best route to political empowerment and economic uplift. While both commented on the spirituals in their writings, DuBois in particular underscored the importance of black worship to cultural identity—calling it, "the Music, the Preaching, and the Frenzy"—and placed the spiritual above all other American contributions to world culture.

At first glance, it may seem that stress upon the primacy of Dr. Watts undermines the claims of critics such as DuBois, Henry Krehbiel, and John Lovell, who persuasively argued the black origins of the spiritual. However, all three wrote during a period of American cultural development when all realms of black experience were, at best, contested. Following upon Epstein's refutation of the white origins theory, other scholars from many disciplines have established beyond question the African roots and American distinctiveness of slave culture. Upon the premise that the basis of slave musical culture was African cultural memory, it is important that we closely examine the Dr. Watts tradition for its seminal role in creating a musical intersection between blacks and whites on North American soil.[18]

While there is a degree of parity between the dispersion of this hymn singing tradition among black and white Primitive Baptists, most telling is the state of worship among Missionary Baptists who comprise the largest black denomination in the United States. Whereas virtually no white Missionary Baptists continue the lining out practice, it persists among their rural and urban black counterparts throughout the country. This suggests the relevance of the practice in terms that are both cultural, social, and musical. Still, many black Baptists have also dispensed with the practice and either turned toward gospel music, focused upon Western European sacred tradition, or developed in both directions. Despite this inexorable drumbeat of social change, traditional hymn singing survives among many Primitive Baptists and other black worshippers because of its primacy in the early development of black performance styles. Its most far-reaching significance in Alabama and elsewhere is that these regional styles contain basic conceptual approaches to music-making which have been recycled and refined in subsequent forms of black music—from spirituals, to blues, to gospel, to jazz, to rhythm and blues, to rap. This movement back and forth between such dichotomies as sacred and secular, traditional and popular, and rural and urban have charted a winding course especially in the twentieth century. Scholars of black music and perhaps American music in general have yet to find effective ways of talking about musical inter-penetrations between the church and the marketplace. However, a study by Michael Harris of Thomas Dorsey, the bluesman who founded black gospel, moves assuredly in this direction.[19] Dorsey's method of melodic transformation exemplifies the interconnections between Dr. Watts singing, blues, and black gospel. John Work foresaw these very same continuities which have proliferated between black Dr. Watts hymn-singing styles and the multiplex of American popular forms when he noted the "melismatic flavor characterizing the singing style of Negro folk music" in the 1940s—which was indeed "derived from these earlier 'Dr. Watts'." No matter how slow, the winds of change are constant and inexorable. Nevertheless, the archaic ideal of the old way of hymn singing continues among Primitive Baptists in general and among black Primitive Baptists in particular as a marker of Christian identity.

Given the politics of race in American heritage, it has been and even now remains difficult to think clearly of originality as a personal and social quest for identity. This sense of a creative impulse may not have much at all to do with the old notion of black and white origins. Paradoxically, the greatest originality may be heard in performances such as "Wondrous Love" which are of apparent Anglo-American "origin." In this kind of transformation, the recognizable essence of the text and melody are retained, but the curve of lyrical melody is sacrificed, not so much for rhythms, in and of themselves, but for the rhythmic incantation of speech. For, in the African tendencies of African American music, musical utterance is governed first by speech and then by movement. Where incantation of a certain spoken text dominates the ritual moment, the power of chant is invoked, and tones serve to intensify or even modify the meaning of words. In most of the hymns recorded in Alabama among black Primitive Baptists, the focus upon texts gave rise to the freely measured moaning sound of languid and malleable speech rhythms. By contrast, usually at an advanced stage of the performance, short, repetitive words and rhythms forge an African association between tempo acceleration and spirit possession which often supplants the early emphasis upon speech rhythms with the more percussive incantations of the ring shout style. These twin poles of moaning and shouting anchor the style continuum heard in the hymn singing of black Primitive Baptists.

#263, "What wondrous love is this" (P.M.)

As sung by Amanda Smith and Ella Pearl While, Loachapoka, Alabama

All transcriptions by W.T. Dargan and copied by C.E. Flowe, Jr.
In phrases intoned by the leader in #3, #241, #364, and #440, each measure stands for the relative temporal space occupied by the sound of one syllable.

#440, "The day is past and gone" (S.M.)

As sung by New Jerusalem Primitive Baptist Church, Bessemer, Alabama

#3, "Amazing grace, how sweet the sound" (C.M.)

As sung by Jesse Allison and Vera Hall, Livingston, Alabama

Moan preceding Hymn #364

#364, "Father, I stretch my hands to thee" (C.M.)

#364 (continued)

As sung by Bethlehem Primitive Baptist Church, Eutaw, Alabama

#382, "While sorrows encompass me round" (8s and 11s)

As sung by Mt. Hebrew Primitive Baptist Church, Notasulga, Alabama

#695, "Dark and thorny is the desert" (8s and 7s)

As sung by Shiloh Primitive Baptist Association, North Carolina, Virginia, Kentucky

#241, "That doleful night before his death" (C.M.)

As sung by Mt. Pilgrim Baptist Church, Livingston, Alabama

Notes

[1] The eight hymns discussed in this article are included on the accompanying CD, including #440, "The day is past and gone"; #695, "Dark and thorny is the desert"; #270, "O may I worthy prove to see"; #3, "Amazing grace how sweet the sound"; #241, "That doleful night before his death"; #263, "What wondrous love is this"; #382, "While sorrows encompass me round"; and #364, "Father, I stretch my hands to thee."

[2] See Mechal Sobel, *Trabelin' On: The Slave Journey to an Afro-Baptist Faith* (Westport, Conn.: Greenwood Press., 1979).

[3] George Pullen Jackson, *White and Negro Spirituals: Their Life Span and Kinship* (Locust Valley, N.Y.: J. J. Augustin, 1943).

[4] Dena Epstein, "A White Origin for the Black Spiritual? An Invalid Theory and How it Grew," *American Music,* 1(1983):53-59.

[5] Daniel Patterson (University of North Carolina at Chapel Hill) brought this similarity to my attention. He is able to see and hear these melodies from such a perspective, not only from his extensive field experience, but from having sung with his students through a number of the tunes published in the *The Sacred Harp*. For this and other possible leads on the relationship between oral and written sources I owe a tremendous debut of gratitude to Professor Patterson.

[6] Ruth Crawford Seeger, transcription of "Amazing Grace," in Jackson, *White and Negro Spirituals*, inserted at the end of the book.

[7] Eileen Southern, *The Music of Black Americans*, revised 3rd ed. (New York: W. W. Norton, 1997); Dena Epstein, *Sinful Tunes and Spirituals: Black Folk Music to the Civil War* (Urbana: University of Illinois Press, 1977).

[8] Richard A. Crawford, *Our American Musical Landscape* (Berkeley: University of California Press, 1993); Samuel A. Floyd, *The Power of Black Music: Interpreting its History from Africa to the United States* (New York: Oxford University Press, 1995).

[9] John W. Work III, "Changing Patterns in Negro Folk Songs," in *Readings in Black American Music*, ed. Eileen Southern, 2nd ed. (New York: W. W. Norton, 1983), 284. Orig. *Journal of American Folklore* 62 (1949): 136-44.

[10] Geneva Smitherman, *Talking and Testifyin': The Language of Black America* (Detroit: Wayne State University Press, 1986), 134-35.

[11] Moaning is a key source for the "blue-note" sound of singing "between the notes" centering around the 3rd, 5th, and 7th degrees of the major scale. Such gestures stem from the slave worship tradition of moaning-prayer and moaning-sermon events, such as those discussed in Willie Collins, "The Moan-and-Prayer Event in African-American Worship," in *In the Spirit: Alabama's Sacred Music Traditions*, ed. Henry Willett, (Montgomery, Alabama: Black Belt Press, 1995).

[12] Various forms of African American "shouting" extend from the African tradition of circle dances directed toward ancestors or gods and increasing in tempo throughout. Whereas African and early African American worship culminated in spirit possession of the celebrant by a deity, in Christian terms, the third Person of the Trinity, the Holy Spirit, indwells the believer and inspires the shouting. In areas such as Brazil, Trinidad, Haiti, and Cuba, continuing worship practices more thoroughly syncretize African and European worship traditions. Nevertheless, as an evocation of the Holy Spirit often complemented by singing and percussive sounds, the African heritage of rhythmic movement continues unabated in North America.

[13] Walter F. Pitts, *Old Ship of Zion: The Afro-Baptist Ritual in the African Diaspora* (New York: Oxford University Press, 1993).

[14] Collins, 22-30.

[15] Epstein, *Sinful Tunes and Spirituals*; Sterling Stuckey, *Slave Culture: Nationalist Theory and the Foundations of Black America* (New York and London: Oxford University Press, 1987).

[16] See Southern, ed., *Readings in Black American Music*, 27-30.
[17] Southern, ed., *Readings in Black American Music*, 62-64.
[18] On the impact of African cultural memory on slave musical culture, see Floyd, *The Power of Black Music*, 8-9.
[19] Michael W. Harris, *The Rise of Gospel Blues: The Music of Thomas Andrew Dorsey in the Urban Church* (New York: Oxford University Press, 1992).

BENJAMIN LLOYD: A PIONEER PRIMITIVE BAPTIST IN ALABAMA

OLIVER C. WEAVER, JR.

Four and a half miles north of Greenville, on the east side of Fort Dale Road, a small family cemetery marks the location of what was once the Lloyd plantation of Butler County, Alabama. Dominating the spot is a monument to Benjamin Lloyd, who bought the place in 1857, immediately moved into a position of leadership in the area, and died prematurely three years later.[1]

By the standards of his day Benjamin Lloyd was a man of wealth, having acquired his competence through such diverse activities as merchant, planter, land speculator, and, at the apex of his career, public official. In his own eyes, however, he was primarily a "Baptist clergyman."[2] A founding father of the Beulah Association of the Primitive Baptist Church, and for twenty-five years a leading minister of that denomination, he served his church well as pastor, moderator, and editor and publisher of its hymnal.

Born October 6, 1804 in Hancock County, Georgia, Benjamin Lloyd spent his infancy on a typical frontier farm of that era. Most of his nearest neighbors were, like the Lloyds, small planters, Baptists, and settlers from Virginia. In childhood and early youth he lived in Jones County, to which his parents moved during his infancy; in later youth he resided in Bibb County, where his family made their home in the early 1820's.[3] In 1822, at the age of eighteen, he was baptized and received into the membership of the Mount Pisgah Baptist Church in Bibb County, Georgia.[4] For the next five years he worked with his father and brothers who, with a dozen slaves, operated several farms in the area. In 1827 he moved with his parents to the newly opened lands of Talbot County, Georgia.

The year 1832 was a climactic one for Benjamin Lloyd. Early in January he purchased a farm in Talbot County and became a planter in his own right. On February 22, 1832 he married Naomi Ann Cox of Putnam County, Georgia.[5] In late autumn his father, John E. Lloyd, Sr., died, leaving Benjamin and his brother the task of administering the estate. On December 27 John Franklyn Lloyd, first of the nineteen children of Benjamin and Naomi, was born.[6] This year, 1832, was also the year of Lloyd's ordination and the commencement of his labors as a minister of the gospel.[7]

Benjamin Lloyd's first ministerial labors occurred within the bounds of the Columbus Association of Georgia. Organized in 1829, this association had been founded on the Articles of Faith of the Flint River Association and was thus committed in principle to the faith espoused by regular Baptists. Extremely conservative in its formative period, the Columbus Association in 1831 repudi-

This article first appeared in the *Alabama Review* 21 (April 1968): 144–55. It is reprinted here with the permission of the University of Alabama Press.

ated the Georgia Baptist Convention and became "disposed to stand aloof from all benevolent enterprises maintained and defended by that body."[8] Although trends toward a more liberal position shortly became manifest, leading the Columbus Association to join the Georgia State Convention in 1838, its earlier conservative views set the tone for Benjamin Lloyd's ministry.

There was another respect, also, in which the Columbus Association proved to be influential upon Lloyd's later career. In 1833, Elder John M. Gray, who had played a prominent role in the 1831 proceedings of the Association, conducted a preaching mission in East Alabama, which laid the foundation upon which Benjamin Lloyd was shortly to build. A later historian of Baptist activities in east Alabama states:

> The first Baptist preachers of whom any trace is found who preached in what is now Chambers County were John M. Gray and Thomas Granbury. They made a tour through east Alabama in the year 1833, and one of their appointments was at Chambersville (now LaFayette), the county seat. The meeting was held in a log cabin used as a court house and church, and a few persons yet live who remember the occasion as one of interest. This was the first religious service conducted in the county by Baptists.[9]

This historian also points out that about the year 1834 other Baptist preachers located in the "Creek country" of Alabama. Among them he names Benjamin Lloyd.

Joey Brackner

Lloyd family cemetery near Greenville, Alabama

Early in 1834 Benjamin Lloyd disposed of his properties in Georgia preparatory to moving across the Chattahoochee River into Alabama. Apparently he did not immediately move his family to Alabama, for his second son, Cary Chappell Lloyd, was born April 2, 1834 in Georgia. His first land acquisition in Alabama came in December, 1834 when he bought a farm in Chambers County. Three months later, on March 24, 1835, his third son, Joseph LaFayette Lloyd, was born in Chambers County, Alabama.

Lloyd's first years in Alabama were characterized by great energy and varied activities. In partnership with his brother Joseph he established one of the early mercantile firms of Chambers County. Under the trade name of "B. Lloyd and Bro.," it was located in LaFayette "next door to Stephen Daniel's tavern."[10] In 1835 he also began a series of land speculations that continued throughout the decade. More than thirty entries in Chambers County deed books are recorded in his name during this period. Almost immediately after his removal to Alabama, Lloyd began preaching among the Baptists of the area. On May 2, 1835, he was one of three elders constituting the presbytery that approved the establishment of County Line Baptist Church.[11]

In the spring of 1836, his career was briefly interrupted by fears of an Indian uprising in East Alabama. The Indians, who had suffered greatly from settlers pressing in upon their lands, were in a hostile mood. On April 1, they killed a white settler, causing a general panic. Wives and children of the settlers were sent across the river into Georgia while the men were organized into military companies. As the general scare spread into nearby Tallapoosa County, settlers gathered in Dudleyville and sent a call for aid to neighbors in Chambers County. As one of the participants in these events wrote many years later:

> A call was at once made for volunteers, and about twenty of us who had horses volunteered our services. We organized by electing the Reverend Benjamin Lloyd, who was an excellent military officer, our captain, and marched off for Dudleyville. We arrived there about sunset and were kindly received by the men who had remained there to protect their property, who provided ample supplies both for us and our horses.[12]

As it turned out, no military action was required during the night, and members of Lloyd's voluntary company returned to their homes the next day.

The autumn of 1836 was a great season for Benjamin Lloyd. He played an active part in organizing the Liberty Association of Baptist churches in east Alabama. He was accorded a place of prominence and influence during the first session of the Liberty Association, which met from September 29 through October 2, 1836 at LaFayette. The Association elected him clerk of the session, appointed him to a committee to write a circular letter to all associated churches, named him correspondent to the Columbus Association of Georgia, and invited him to preach the introductory sermon to the Liberty Association a year hence. Along with these honors, the Association paid him twenty dollars for his services as clerk of the session.[13]

Scarcely had the session ended when Lloyd was invited by the Cusseta Church to become its pastor. A similar invitation came from the church at

LaFayette, and he accepted both.[14] During the organization of the Liberty Association there seems to have been little overt division between Primitive and Missionary Baptists. In fact, the Association attempted to establish itself on a foundation broad enough to include both and so to avoid the divisions that were already a source of much friction among Georgia Baptists. Reflecting the earlier conservative sentiment of the Columbus Association, however, Liberty adopted a compromise resolution weighted somewhat on the anti-missionary side. Article VII of its constitution provided that "the Association shall not engage in the missionary institutions of the day but leave churches and individuals to exercise their judgment in such cases."[15]

Although Lloyd doubtless preferred an even more severe stand than that embodied in Article VII, he accepted it and remained with the Liberty Association through its second year. Illness prevented his preaching the introductory sermon at the second session of the Liberty Association, which commenced September 23, 1837, but he was again elected clerk of the session. His connection with Liberty, however, ended shortly thereafter. His name appears nowhere in the minutes of the third session, in 1838. A year later, in 1839, the Association minutes carried only one reference to him, noting that the new clerk had "made a settlement with Benjamin Lloyd, former clerk, and received of him $2.94, but said Lloyd had not procured a record book for the Association." Although no reason for Lloyd's separation from the Liberty Association was explicitly given, the occasion for his departure may be easily inferred from item 23 of the minutes, namely, that the Association unanimously adopted repeal of Article VII of the constitution and now urged all churches to send contributions to missionary causes throughout the Association. The fact that this position was unanimously adopted indicates that not only Lloyd but all of his fellow anti-missionary conservatives had withdrawn.

McGinty's *History of the East Liberty Baptist Association* throws a bit of additional light on this. After noting that Lloyd was chosen pastor of the Cusseta Church in 1836, McGinty added: "He [Lloyd] also intimated in a private way, after one year as pastor, the propriety of the church declaring non-fellowship for missionary causes, but he was firmly opposed by the brethren whom he approached on the subject."[16]

His experience with the LaFayette Baptist Church was similar. Late in 1838, Lloyd and fellow Baptists who had departed from the Liberty Association with him founded the Beulah Association of Primitive Baptist Church. As one of the founders of the Beulah Association, Lloyd moved immediately into a place of leadership among the Primitive Baptists comparable to that which he had formerly enjoyed in the Liberty Association. Minutes prior to 1842 are missing, but in September of that year, he preached the introductory sermon to the Beulah Association on the text, "Giving no offense in anything that the ministry be not blamed."[17] He served on several committees and as correspondent to various associations, including the Ebenezer (Alabama) Association. He became pastor of various Primitive Baptist churches in Chambers County, including the church at Sharon and the church at Fredonia, the latter town being his place of residence for several years. In the mid-1840s, he moved to Coosa County, where he served as preacher of the Primitive Baptist Church in east Wetumpka.

In 1845, with the organization of the Wetumpka Association of the Primitive Baptist Church, Benjamin Lloyd preached within the new Association, but for more than a decade while living in and around Wetumpka, he also continued his active interest in the affairs of the Beulah Association. Minutes of the latter show that from 1845 to 1857 he attended the annual meetings of the Beulah Association, usually as correspondent from the Wetumpka Association. It was almost a regular routine for him to give the opening prayer and to preach either a Saturday morning or a Saturday morning or a Saturday afternoon sermon before the Beulah Association.[18] As far as posterity is concerned, his chief claim to fame during these years was his publication of Lloyd's *Primitive Hymns*. This hymnal, which has now been in use by the Primitive Baptist churches for more than a century and a quarter, was first published in 1841. The last edition was in 1963.[19]

During the decade in which he lived in Coosa County, Benjamin Lloyd established his home on the famous Old Plank Road some twelve miles north of Wetumpka, near the Central Institute.[20] This Missionary Baptist Institute, the ranking academy of the county, was probably the school in which his younger children received a substantial portion of their education. During these years, Lloyd seems to have mellowed in his opposition to the Missionary Baptists, and he enjoyed the esteem of many people in the community. A character sketch of him, written by a Missionary Baptist preacher, was as follows:

> Coosa has been the home of men who have taken places of distinction in the ministry of the gospel. Reverend Benjamin Lloyd, who came from Chambers County, lived for some years in Coosa. He was a minister of the Primitive Baptist denomination. His early history is unknown to the writer except that he was from South Carolina. He was a man of medium size and carrying a face that would strike the beholder as denoting intelligence, refinement and a gentle spirit. He was much above most of the ministers of that denomination for education. He was the compiler and publisher of their Primitive Hymnbook which was a good source of revenue to him and to his family after his death. He had moved from Coosa to Butler before the war and died there. He and his wife had sixteen sons and four daughters. Several of his sons became ministers, most of them missionary preachers of good standing. The humorous writer [Francis Bartow Lloyd] so well known in Alabama as "Rufus Sanders" was of his family a grandson.[21]

That Benjamin Lloyd was a man of some standing in his community is evidence by the fact that in 1857 he was appointed by President James Buchanan as Receiver of Public Monies for the Land Office located at Greenville, Alabama. Upon receipt of this appointment, he purchased a plantation in Butler County, some four and one-half miles north of Greenville, moved his family there, and immediately entered upon the duties of his office. He continued, however, an active role as a Primitive Baptist minister and managed the affairs of his new plantation. He also ran the hotel at Fort Dale.[22]

Serving as pastor of the Primitive Baptist Church of Fort Dale and also of the church at Mount Zion in Butler County, Lloyd assumed a place of leadership in the Ebenezer Association of the Primitive Baptist Church.[23] In September of 1859 he was elected as Moderator of the Association, was requested to write a circular letter to all of the churches, and was also named as correspondent to the Wetumpka Association.

The circular letter that Benjamin Lloyd wrote to the churches of the Ebenezer Association confirms Brewer's characterization of him as a man of refinement and gentle spirit. Avoiding doctrinal discussion as inappropriate to a circular letter, he aimed, rather, to incite the members of the Association "to love and to good works." At the outset of his comments, however, he stressed most strongly the nature of the Church. "The Holy Scriptures," he wrote, "present to view in the Church of Christ a peculiar people, separate and distinct from all the world besides, people united to God, having been taught by His spirit and brought into fellowship and communion with Him."[24]

True to his Baptist heritage and to his understanding of the gospel, he stressed a kind of democracy in the church, the equality of all men before God—ministers and laity alike. "The Gospel," he wrote, "recognizes no distinction of subjects." Nevertheless, there are distinct duties for the congregation and other duties for ministers. Only ministers have the right and the authority to administer baptism and the Lord's Supper. Having accepted the office of pastor of a church, a minister has the responsibility for tending his flock, for visiting among his people, for knowing which of his members are "vacillating upon any subject" in order that he might "establish them." Reflecting, I think, the political traditions of the post-revolutionary period in American history, he also stressed the role of the minister in conducting the affairs of conferences. "Here moves are to be made and seconded and the vote to be taken," he said. "Every church," he wrote, "should have a proper decorum in which the duties of every member should be defined; and in all cases where members desire to speak on any subject, they should rise from their seats." Benjamin Lloyd was a practical man, and he knew from firsthand experience some of the problems of making democracy work—even ecclesiastical democracy.

In his circular letter, Lloyd discussed the duties of all Christians to attend services of worship and the ordinances of the church, to contribute to the church's support, and to pray in the church as well as in the family circle. He discussed at some length duties and authority of deacons, stressing their obligations "by kindly effort to restore to peace any little disturbances among the members." All in all, his circular letter reflects the mood and concerns of a pastor on the Alabama frontier for the practical, everyday tasks of maintaining the church and properly administering its ordinances.

Scarcely had Lloyd completed this circular letter when he, though still only fifty-five years old, was stricken with an illness from which he never recovered. On January 9, 1860 he drew his will, recording previous gifts to his older children, leaving $1,000 each to ten of his children who were still minors, providing for the disposition of many items of personal property (including his numerous slaves), and directing his executors to renew the copyright and continue publication of his "Primitive Hymns."[25] On January 14, 1860, after an illness of two months, he died. His career, like that of many other preachers of the American frontier, is a vivid reminder of the fact that the cultural traditions through which man's ancient faiths have been renewed from generation to generation are transmitted in part, but only in part, by the written word.

On the American frontier, pioneer preachers frequently owned little more reading material than a Bible and a hymnal, their parishioners often possessing neither of these. Nevertheless, ancient forms of the faith took root and flourished on American soil—transmitted largely through oral communication, through sermon and song, through sacrament and symbol. The life of Benjamin Lloyd reflects the convictions of a Primitive Baptist preacher as he tried to make a living and carry Christianity to a frontier people.

Notes

[1] The author of this paper is indebted to Mrs. Eugene S. Bee, Special Collections Librarian, Samford University, for her assistance in locating source materials. All of the minutes cited in this paper can be found on microfilm in the Special Collections of the Harwell G. Davis Library of Samford University.

[2] He was listed in this manner in the 1850 United States Manuscript Census for Coosa County, Alabama.

[3] Benjamin Lloyd's grandfather, John Lloyd, came to Georgia from Virginia after the Revolutionary War. On the tenth of September, 1784, he received a warrant for two hundred acres of land on Beaver Dam Creek near the Waters of Ogeechee. The farm bordered "Greenbury Road" and was situated three miles west of Powellton in Hancock County, Georgia. Following the grandfather's death in October, 1793, the farm was managed by Benjamin's father, John E. Lloyd, until it was sold to Colonel Henry T. Colquitt in 1807. Records of transactions pertaining to it can be found in Wilkes County, Georgia, land Grant Book A, 6; Greene County, Georgia, Estate Books A and B, 216-218. Deed books of Jones, Bibb, and Talbot counties, Georgia, provided evidence of the places of residence of John E. Lloyd. He is listed in the United Manuscript Census for Jones County, Georgia, in 1820, and Talbot County, Georgia, in 1830.

[4] "Obituary" in Minutes of the Twenty-Third Annual Session of the Ebenezer Baptist Association of the Primitive Faith and Order. Held with Ebenezer Church, Dallas County, Alabama, from the 5th to the 8th day of October, Inclusive, 1860.

[5] Putnam County, Georgia, Marriage Book D, 218.

[6] The date is given in the family Bible of Benjamin Lloyd's son Jesse Cox Lloyd (privately owned). A complete list of children of Benjamin and Naomi Ann (Cox) Lloyd can be found in Thomas M. Owen, *History of Alabama and Dictionary of Alabama Biography* (Chicago, 1921), 4:1056. Partial lists can be found in the Manuscript Census for Coosa County, Alabama, 1850, and for Butler County, Alabama, 1860, the latter listing Naomi A. Lloyd as head of the household.

[7] "Obituary."

[8] J. H. Campbell, *Georgia Baptists: Historical and Biographical* (Macon, Georgia: 1874), 100.

[9] W. C. Bledsoe, *History of the Liberty (East) Baptist Association of Alabama* (Atlanta: 1886), 8. While on this preaching tour, Elder John M. Gray died in Alabama "at Mr. Pittman's place," an event noted in the minutes of the Columbus Association in 1834. See Campbell, 102. A more recent account of Gray and his mission in Alabama states: "Elder Gray was one of the presbytery who helped organize that LaFayette Baptist Church in May, 1834. In July of the same year he was taken ill while preaching in the community in which the Bethel Church was organized and died, being a victim of typhoid fever, according to records found in the library of Mercer University, Macon Georgia. He had served the First Baptist Church of Columbus, Georgia, as pastor and had organized the first church at Macon, Georgia." B. B. McGinty, *History of East Liberty Baptist Association, Chambers County, Alabama* (Alexander City, Alabama: 1963), 2.

[10] E. G. Richard, "Reminiscences of the Early Days in Chambers County," *Alabama*

Historical Quarterly 4 (Fall 1942): 432. See also Chambers County, Alabama, Deed Book 1, 42.

[11] McGinty, 205-206.

[12] Richards, 440.

[13] Minutes of the Liberty Baptist Association Constituted at LaFayette, Chambers County, Alabama, September 28, 1836.

[14] McGinty, 208, 216.

[15] Minutes of the Liberty Baptist Association (1836).

[16] McGinty, 208.

[17] Minutes of the Fifth Session of the Beulah Baptist Association, Meeting with the Church at Sharon, Chambers County, Alabama, September 17-20, 1842, Inclusive.

[18] See Minutes for each year, 1846 through 1857.

[19] The writer is indebted to F. Wilbur Helmbold, Director of the Harwell G. Davis Library of Samford University, for the following information: Following the first edition of 1841 there were editions of 1845, 1858, 1869, 1876, 1900, 1921, and later. The 1845 edition was published by J. F. Trow, printer, 38 Ann Street, New York. It carried the inscription: "The Primitive hymns, spiritual songs, and sacred poems, regularly selected, classified, and set in order, and adapted to social singing and all occasions of divine worship—Third edition, corrected and enlarged. Published for the proprietor, and for sale by him at Wetumpka, Alabama, 1845." Recent editions, including that of 1963, carry a frontispiece portrait of Benjamin Lloyd. [Ed.: Weaver's edition information, of course, was incomplete and does not include editions printed after the publication of his article. For the most comprehensive listing of *Primitive Hymns* editions, see Joey Brackner, "The Primitive Hymns: Descriptions of Extant Editions" in this volume.]

[20] George Evans Brewer, "History of Coosa County," *Alabama Historical Quarterly* 4 (Spring 1942): 81.

[21] Ibid., 216-217. The comment of Brewer cited above is apparently in error in stating that Benjamin Lloyd was from South Carolina. Benjamin's father, John Lloyd, lived in Pendleton District, South Carolina, briefly about 1790, and his wife's parents, Cary and Martha (Rountree) Cox, lived in Edgefield District in the decade 1790-1800, but no evidence has been found that Benjamin Lloyd lived there. Another minor point: Brewer mentions twenty children. Family records preserve the names of only nineteen.

[22] Copy of a letter from Mrs. Walter Henry Crenshaw to Edward Crenshaw, June 27, 1857, provided by Mrs. Richard Crenshaw of Greenville, Alabama.

[23] Minutes of Mt. Zion Church, Butler County, Alabama, dated Friday, July 9, 1958 declare: "The church went into the choice of a supply pastor to fill the vacancy of Brother W. Thomas. She made choice of Brother Benjamin Lloyd.—The Church agreed to commune the next sabbath and wash one another's feet." Minutes of Saturday, November 13, 1858 state: "The church went into the choice of a pastor for the year 1859. They made choice of Brother Benjamin Lloyd."

[24] Benjamin Lloyd, "Circuclar Letter" in Minutes of the Twenty-Second Annual Session of the Ebenezer Baptist Association Meeting in the Bethlehem Church, Montgomery County, from the 3rd to the 6th of September, 1859. The quotations following that cited above are also from this circular letter. [Ed.: Weaver might have adjusted his depiction of the circular letter as a kind of charter of Lloyd's theological posture had he known about other writings in religious periodicals. Joey Brackner has discovered that Lloyd was a regular contributor to *Primitive Baptist*, *Signs of the Times*, and *The Southern Baptist Messenger* where he marketed his book and wrote on the state of the church.]

[25] Butler County, Alabama, Will Book 1, 146. The will was dated January 9, 1860 and probated March 5, 1860.

Naomi A. Lloyd

ELDER BENJAMIN LLOYD AND HIS HYMN BOOK

JOEY BRACKNER

In 1841, Benjamin Lloyd, a Primitive Baptist elder from Chambers County, Alabama, published *The Primitive Hymns, Spiritual Songs, and Sacred Poems, Regularly Selected, Classified and Set in Order And Adapted to Social Singing and all Occasions of Divine Worship*. Known simply as "Lloyd's Hymn Book" or "Primitive Hymns," this text-only hymn book is a time marker for the advent of the Primitive Baptist denomination and was kept in print by the descendants of the Lloyd family for one hundred and thirty years. The Primitive Hymns Corporation of Rocky Mount, North Carolina, currently prints it in facsimile of the 1921 edition. Primitive Baptist churches throughout the United States have clung to this book as a familiar companion in worship and a connection to the past. More recently, the national revival of Sacred Harp singing has recognized *Primitive Hymns* as a document both connected to the development of shape note singing and representative of an antecedent tradition. As such, *Primitive Hymns* is a continuing force in American folk music. Elder Lloyd would be very surprised by, delighted in, and no doubt humbled by the interest in his book at the turn of the millennium.

The Origins and Development of the Tradition

Metered, unaccompanied, congregational singing from text-only hymn books is the South's earliest form of non-aboriginal religious music and was even adopted by many of the state's Indian groups prior to their removal in the 1830s. This practice dates back to the reformation in the Old World and therefore predates the advent of Primitive Baptists in the New World. The retention of this style of unaccompanied singing using text-only hymn books such as *Primitive Hymns* is in part a statement of religious doctrine setting Primitive Baptists apart from those Baptists and other denominations that do not accept the doctrine of predestined salvation by grace. This musical preference is based on scriptural interpretations and an ongoing debate about the role of musical instruments in church that dates back to John Calvin. This is also why so many Primitive Baptists also participate in the all-vocal shape note traditions of the South that were developing at the time of the first edition of *Primitive Hymns*.

The man who set the standard for generations of hymn books was Isaac Watts (1674-1748), considered by some the "originator of modern church hymns."[1] Watts was born to a family of dissenters and non-conformists in Southampton, England. As a minister, he wrote many hymns, forty-four of which were based on his sermons, such as "Alas and did my Saviour bleed."[2] This began the practice of "homiletical hymnody," whereby hymn texts were selected to echo the theme of a sermon. To facilitate this practice, Watts organized his hymn book, *Hymns and Spiritual Songs*, with sections combining hymns with common themes so that a pastor could easily select a hymn appropriate for an occasion or message.[3] This reference-oriented structure was copied in later hymn collections including that of Benjamin Lloyd, who organized segments of his hymn book for such occasions as "Lord's Supper," "Washing the Saints Feet," and "Dismission." In the preface of the first edition of *Primitive Hymns*, Lloyd wrote: "In this book, I have arranged the Hymns and spiritual Songs under different heads, or classes. And have pursued that order which appeared to me to agree with the plan of salvation, and the effect and progress of the gospel and the teachings of the Holy Spirit, by which the dear children of God are brought to a knowledge of the truth, and led to the ordinances of the gospel, and enabled to walk in them to the glory of their heavenly Father. 'And all thy children shall be taught of the Lord, and great shall be the peace of thy children.' "

Congregational singing in Baptist churches in England in the late seventeenth century set the stage for this form of worship among eighteenth century Baptists in the southern Atlantic colonies of America.[4] Watts' hymnals were very popular among non-Anglicans in England and later in colonial America. In America, the animosity between the Anglican Church and dissenting groups mirrored that of England. Baptists in the colonial American South continued to be at odds with Anglican authority. They objected to a state-sponsored church and consequently refused to pay for preaching licenses. They also felt that Anglican doctrine was too comfortable and "dangerously" complacent.[5] On the other hand, Anglicans feared that Baptists would undermine local authority and challenge the social class structure. Anglicans in the colonial south were suspicious of and ridiculed Baptist rituals such as laying on of hands, baptism by immersion, or footwashing.[6] This persecution by and suspicion of government and other controlling societies and institutions would later help shape the differences and disagreements among Baptists.

Although Primitive Baptists today consider theirs the original Baptist church, their beliefs are not identical with early Baptist churches in America whose heterogeneity gave birth to both the Primitive and Missionary Baptists. Indeed, "divisiveness" and doctrinal disputes have characterized Baptists and their antecedents since the seventeenth century.[7] One common area of disagreement has been the circumstances of salvation. After Calvin's death, the nature of "predestination," the determination of who was "destined" for heaven or hell, was debated. The solution of the English Puritans was the theology of particular atonement, the idea that, since the beginning of time, God has already determined who will be saved. Dutch Remonstrants, under Jacob Arminius, softened this stance by their suggestion that salvation was predestined by "God's foreknowledge of an individual's faith." In the eighteenth century, a set of beliefs developed among English Baptists that rejected this "Arminianism," emphasized predestination, and de-emphasized the role of the individual in salvation.[8] This "hyper-Calvinism" set the stage for the schism that developed over the mission controversy of the early nineteenth century because the emerging Primitive Baptists would later assert "Christ died only for the elect, therefore, evangelism is not necessary."[9]

Historically, the early Baptists did not give much financial support to their elders, therefore the financial concerns of a church were relatively simple.[10] The issue of money was another part of the objection that some Baptists had in supporting missions in the early nineteenth century. Support for such efforts meant raising money and appointing people to distribute these funds. The suspicion of any "centralizing authority" as well as an aversion to the collection of money were a basis for anti-mission sentiment among these Baptists.[11] The position of Baptist churches that disapproved of supporting "tract societies, Sunday schools, bible societies, missions, theological schools, sectarian colleges and protracted meetings" was expressed through the Kehukee Declaration (North Carolina, 1827) and the Black Rock Address (Maryland, 1833). These documents and the views they expressed became the texts through which these Baptist churches, soon to be known as Primitive Baptist, began disassociating themselves from other Baptists.[12] The Primitive Baptists developed a doctrine that considered any form of centralized church government to be unacceptable.[13]

Music was to become another field upon which the emerging Primitive Baptists would set themselves apart from others and where Benjamin Lloyd would make his mark. Singing was an important part of the Great Awakening, and appreciated by people as much as, if not more than, the sermons. John Leland wrote of 1790 Virginia that "singing was more blessed among the people than the preaching."[14] What was the character of this singing? One characteristic may have been the "lining" of hymns. In the eighteenth century, John Rippon discouraged the practice of "reading line by line," known today as "lining" or "lining out" a hymn.[15] In this process, someone would read a line from a hymn and then the congregation would sing the same line. Rippon's protest suggests that "lining" was already a very old tradition among Baptists, perhaps borne of necessity since there was little money to buy hymnals for everyone and besides, many could not read. Some figures suggest that 20% of the white population in the South were illiterate as late as 1850.[16]

In New England, Puritans also sang this way until some congregations started using printed music. Other congregations continued singing the "old way." This movement to use printed music and conduct "singing schools" was a development that eventually came to the South. The southern manifestation became what is referred to as "shape note" singing and introduced harmony into what had been melody-only hymn singing. "Tunebooks," wedding well-known hymn lyrics with musical notation, were published in the South in the early nineteenth century. By the time Benjamin Lloyd published his hymn book, this new sound of hymn singing may have affected the way people sang, even out of text-only books.

The use of musical instruments became another area of disagreement among Baptists. Early Calvinists would not allow musical instruments, namely the organ, into church.[17] After the Civil War, Missionary Baptist churches began acquiring organs while Primitive Baptists didn't.[18] But in the antebellum era, musical instruments were rare, even in pro-mission Baptist churches.[19] This accounts for the text-only hymnals produced by pro-mission Baptists such as Basil Manley and Jesse Mercer after the schism. The self-conscious resistance by Primitive Baptists to the introduction of musical instruments was true to their conservative nature and added one more point of distinction for their group. Paul Drummond states that to be appropriate for worship, Primitive Baptists music should be sung spiritually, with understanding, congregationally, and unaccompanied. He adds that "spirituality in singing is more important than style or quality of performance."[20] It is, however, both the style and conscious conservatism of their music that have made Primitive Baptists curators of American religious folksong.

Benjamin Lloyd and His Times

An excellent profile of Benjamin Lloyd and details about his life can be found in Oliver C. Weaver's "Benjamin Lloyd: A Pioneer Baptist in Alabama," which is reprinted in this book. Weaver, a descendant of Lloyd, is one of many descendants and/or admirers who have researched the Elder's life and helped spread information about this important man. He is one of the few whose findings have been published. There is, however, much awareness about certain particulars of Lloyd's life and his hymn book in the oral tradition. Among these is the widely known fact that the daguerreotype of a bald man at the front of the modern editions of *Primitive Hymns* is not Elder Lloyd, but instead his father-in-law, Cary Cox. There is an awareness that he was a Georgia native who came into Alabama shortly after statehood. Many know that Benjamin Lloyd and his wife Naomi had nineteen children; that he was a land speculator and was, of course, a Primitive Baptist preacher. Most know that Elder Lloyd died on the eve of the Civil War and that later, three of his sons were lost to that conflict. But perhaps the most compelling bit of common knowledge is that he stipulated in his will for his hymn book to be kept in print for future generations to use and that his descendants were true to his wishes.

Benjamin Lloyd's world was so different than that of the modern South that one hardly knows where to begin with its description. Georgia and especially Alabama were frontiers in the early nineteenth century, and relations with the American Indians were very unsettled on the eve of their removal. Swindlers, armed robbers, poor roads, and disease further added uncertainty to life on the "Old Southwest" frontier. Community leaders such as Benjamin Lloyd helped "civilize" and bring order to a violent frontier, difficult by almost any standard. Against this stressful backdrop was the effort of settlers to establish churches and conduct their lives according to the scriptures.

There was a diversity of persons who came into the Alabama frontier during the early nineteenth century, but most were of modest means. Those who professed any religious affiliation were most likely Baptists or Methodists. According to Hosea Holcombe, Alabama had about fifty Baptist churches at the time of statehood in 1819. By 1840, there were 30 associations and about 500 Baptist churches.[21] This wave of Baptists made relevant to most of the population the brewing disagreement over the mission question, which raged from 1817 until 1837.[22] Benjamin Lloyd first preached in the Columbus Association of Georgia prior to his emigration to Alabama. At that time, the Columbus Association opposed the Georgia Baptist Convention and its perceived "liberal" notions. Like many other Associations, it later (1838) softened its opposition to a statewide organization that also acknowledged tract and missionary societies but "its earlier conservative views set the tone for Benjamin Lloyd's ministry."[23]

Lloyd followed the lead of Elder John Gray and moved into the "Creek Country" of Chambers County, Alabama, in 1834.[24] He lived first in the Mount Hickory community and later moved to Wickerville. In 1836, Lloyd, his brother Joseph, and William Graggs established a store, "B. Lloyd and Bro." in

LaFayette.[25] He also began land speculating. The earliest land tract book for Chambers County is full of transactions involving Benjamin Lloyd. One of the earliest of these records shows Elder Lloyd acquiring a portion of land in 1835. In 1840, another transaction brought land from an Indian named Spoke-Oke-harjo into Lloyd's possession. One of the last of Elder Lloyd's transactions in Chambers County, entered on June 30, 1841, was for land from an Indian named No-Cou-hatch-ee and somehow associated with the "Creek Treaty." Lloyd was elected Captain of a local militia group during the Creek Indian crisis of 1836 and they marched off to Dudleyville. There was no fighting and the group disbanded.[26] Unlike most people in 1830s Chambers County, Benjamin Lloyd's name appears in many official records. Benjamin Lloyd witnessed the will of William Coggins on June 8, 1835.[27] He performed a marriage ceremony for William George and Mary McCoy on March 15, 1838.[28] These documents underscore the stature of Lloyd, who, while only in his thirties, was both a man of means and a pillar of the community.

Baptist churches in the South during the 1830s were small and made of hewn logs like the residences. Many of these had no glass windows. Later, larger frame construction churches were made with thick sawn planks. Many early Baptist churches that still exist show the two entrances, one for women and the other for men. Sometimes side entrances are also present. Some Primitive Baptists still sit segregated by gender during worship. In such churches pews, usually called benches, are arranged on three sides facing inward on a pulpit that is slightly elevated. As one faces the pulpit, the women sit on the left and the men to the right. Visitors face the pulpit. As most do today, Primitive Baptist churches met once a month. In the 1830s, music might provide the bulk of a service in a Primitive Baptist church if no preacher was in attendance. At the Beard's Creek Primitive Baptist Church in south Georgia, the congregation still used one well-worn copy of Mercer's *Cluster* as late as 1838. The "singing clerk" was in charge of the book and lined the hymns.[29]

Benjamin Lloyd helped found and was clerk of the Liberty Association of churches in 1836 where he pastored the LaFayette, County Line, and Cussetta churches.[30] Two years later, he and other anti-mission Baptists from Liberty established the Beulah Association. Their departure was based on the schism over endorsing and supporting missions.[31] Hosea Holcombe in his *History of the Baptists in Alabama* mentions Lloyd in discussing the Liberty Association: "...and Elder B. Lloyd was clerk, for the first two years, but he has gone over to the New Test party." He continues, "The Association [Liberty] is now apparently prospering, yet we may suspect they are not entirely through with their difficulties; as the spirit of schism is amongst them; and if not in their own churches, they are so intermingled, with the churches of the Beulah Association [anti-mission], that we may reasonably look for further difficulties."[32] Holcombe, who cast his lot with the pro-mission Baptists, went on to disparage the Beulah Association: "As there is nothing of much interest in the proceedings of this body; we will make a short extract from their letter of correspondence: 'We must decline all fellowship,' say they, 'for, or correspondence with, such associations and professors of the Baptists, or of any other name, as have departed from the faith and order of the gospel, or as have attempted to add to the divine decree any of the institutions of human inventions, of whatever name they may be called.'"[33] The Beulah formation was on the forefront of a region-wide split among the Baptists. Later, in 1838, seventeen anti-mission churches withdrew from the Alabama Association and formed the Ebenezer Association in south central Alabama.[34] Even though many at the time did not recognize it, the dichotomy of Baptist churches was complete. During this time, Benjamin Lloyd began reading and contributing to periodicals associated with non-mission Baptists.

In the pages of *The Signs of the Times* and *The Primitive Baptist*, one could read letters, statements, and correspondence about the divisions occurring in the Baptist church. *The Primitive Baptist*, a publication from eastern North Carolina made its debut in 1835 issued by the Kehukee Association, an epicenter of anti-mission sentiment. The use of "Primitive Baptist" by this publication reinforced its adoption as the moniker for anti-mission Baptists.[35] Benjamin Lloyd served as an agent for the *Primitive Baptist* during the 1840s and 1850s. These and other publications would later be instrumental in marketing his hymn book. In a letter to the *Primitive Baptist* dated April 9, 1839, Lloyd may have weighed in for the first time in print on the issue of missions. He wrote:

> Dear Brethren: I have sent you a preamble and resolutions, entered into at a meeting of ministers and deacons from several Associations in Georgia and Alabama, of the New School Baptists, their names and appellations accompanying them, for publication for use and benefit of the Primitive Baptists and all others who read this paper, & c. Please give it a place. I am anxious for my brethren to know that these things are so.
>
> Dear Brethren, the circulation of your valuable paper is increasing in this country, and the blessed cause of our Redeemer gaining ground. And may the Lord influence by his Spirit, till the dear children of God shall get clear of the galling yoke of oppression, and realize that blessed freedom spoken of in the scripture: If the Son shall make you free, you shall be free indeed.
>
> Yours in the best of bonds, &c. Benjamin Lloyd

It is interesting to note that Lloyd referred to Missionary Baptists as "New School," while Holcombe called Primitives "New Test." Obviously, both sides were claiming the high ground of being the "old" and, by inference, true church.

The 1840 census taker for Chambers County found Benjamin Lloyd and Naomi with five sons and six slaves in their household. As a businessman and a preacher, Lloyd was providing his community with what they needed both spiritually and materially. These realms converged in 1841 when he published the first edition of *Primitive Hymns*. On March 18, 1841, Benjamin Lloyd sent a letter from Lafayette to be published in the *Primitive Baptist* announcing "that I have made preliminary arrangements for the publication of a Hymn Book adapted to the use of the Old School Baptists.... The Hymns will be classified and embodied under appropriate heads, adapted to singing on all occasions. And in presenting the contemplated work to the public, I do not expect to excel others who have made similar publications; but that duty has

Lloyd's last home, the Palings, near Greenville, Alabama, as it looked in 1935.

for some time rested with weight on my mind, seeing that no one of the Primitive denomination had stepped forward...."[36] Later that year, in a letter to the *Primitive Baptist* dated July 12, he announced that fifteen hundred copies of his hymn book would be available on August 15. Price per book was one dollar.[37]

Soon afterward, in late 1842, Benjamin Lloyd left Chambers County and moved to Coosa County (in what is now Elmore County) and became pastor of the Primitive Baptist church in east Wetumpka.[38] In a letter to the *Primitive Baptist* sent from Wetumpka, Alabama, and dated December 30, 1842, Lloyd wrote: "I have removed to Wetumpka, Ala.... I avail myself of the present opportunity to give an expression of my gratitude and high obligations to the brethren and generous public for their kindness in giving patronage to my Hymn Book, as well as the many expressions of the high estimate placed on my Hymn Book, as well as the many expressions of the high estimate placed on my Hymns, their order and adaptedness, &c. And I would also give notice to the brethren and public, that I am preparing to publish a second edition."[39] He settled near the present town of Central about twelve miles north along the old Plank Road. Central Institute was the major Missionary Baptist school in the area and was the school the Lloyd children most likely attended.[40] The 1850 Census for Coosa County lists Benjamin Lloyd's occupation as "B[aptist] Clergyman" and his holdings in real estate at $1800. His seventeen-year-old son John is listed along with ten younger brothers in his household. John's occupation is listed as farmer. His brother Joseph who lived nearby is listed as a farmer who owns $2500 in real estate. The Lloyds' time in Coosa county was most prolific. Several more children were born and several more editions of *Primitive Hymns* were printed. The most important of these was the third and enlarged edition printed in 1845. It was this version of the hymn book that remained unchanged almost to the end of the nineteenth century.

In 1857, the President of the United States, James Buchanan appointed Lloyd as Receiver of Public Monies at the Greenville Land Office. This appointment precipitated his move to a plantation near Fort Dale just north of Greenville in Butler County.[41] He died three years later on January 14, 1860, and was buried there in the family cemetery on their plantation called the "Palings." In his will, dated January 9, 1860, and entered in the Butler County Will Book office, he stipulated: "It is my will and desire that my executors shall continue to publish my collection of Hymns, known as the 'Primitive Hymns,' renew the copy-right thereof, or else to sell the right—entirely as they may think most beneficial: the proceeds of which are to be disposed of as my other property under this will." Lloyd's family chose the option stipulated in the will for the continuation of his hymn book and, despite the turbulent years ahead, strove to do his bidding.

The following announcement was run in the March 10, 1860, issue of the *Primitive Baptist,* just following Benjamin Lloyd's obituary:

> ***A CIRCULAR TO THE PRIMITIVE BAPTISTS.***
>
> Dear Brethren:
>
> Previous to the death of my husband, Elder Benjamin Lloyd, author of the Primitive Hymns, he requested that his Hymn Book business should be carried on for the accommodation of the Primitive Baptists. His family will carry on the Book business just as it was during his lifetime. We will continue to have the Books published, always keeping a full supply on hand, so that our Agents and friends can order them at any time, and we will be thankful to meet their orders promptly. We hope that all the brethren and friends who have heretofore been acting as agents for the H. Books, will continue to exercise their influence and assistance in our behalf.
>
> Yours Respectfully
> Naomi A. Lloyd.

This announcement was printed with an advertisement listing prices throughout 1860 in the *Primitive Baptist* and the *Southern Baptist Messenger.* This advertisement is not present in the issues of these periodicals that survive from the Civil War years (some from 1861 through 1864). One can surmise that advertising costs and restocking the hymn book was dropped from the Lloyds' wartime budget. Undoubtedly, their prospective customers were also frugal during this time. Nine of Benjamin and Naomi Lloyd's sons served in the Confederate Army.

Historian George Evans Brewer states that Benjamin Lloyd's hymnal "was a good source of revenue for him and for his family after his death."[42] It is certain that the book sold well, but for a family as prosperous as the Lloyds, the publication of the book would have been only a fraction of their income. Therefore, it would be more accurate to consider *Primitive Hymns* as a spiritual rather than financial legacy from Benjamin Lloyd to his descendants.

The Development and Perseverance of the Hymn Book

Primitive Hymns originally had 535 hymns. It was revised and enlarged in 1845 to contain 694 numbered hymns (these same hymns were later renumbered to make a total of 700). Today, the two versions in use contain either these 700 hymns or these and 5 additional hymns. How the book was created, criticized, endured, changed, and then changed back again is an interesting, if incomplete story.

The practice of compiling a hymn book was fairly common for frontier ministers in the early nineteenth century. Many of these men must have felt that "the responsibility for making hymns available for worship rested on the shoulders of the local minister who was familiar with the hymnody of his denomination."[43] By his own account, Benjamin Lloyd "stepped forward" to provide a hymn book for Primitive Baptists after the schism.[44] The choice of *Primitive Hymns* as a title may have boosted the initial popularity of the book and also aided its longevity. But what were the sources for *Primitive Hymns*?

The hymns as printed in Lloyd's book do not offer the names of the authors, though the majority can easily be traced to the canon of eighteenth century English hymns. The absence of author attribution could be interpreted as ambivalence on the part of the compiler, because hymns were considered divinely inspired. Therefore, a human author was merely a vessel through which scriptural interpretation was communicated.[45] Nevertheless, the predominance of English evangelicals in *Primitive Hymns* may be due to the Baptist, John Rippon, who published *A Selection of Hymns from the Best Authors Intended to be an Appendix to Dr. Watts' Psalms and Hymns* in London in 1787. This became the major source for Baptist hymn compilers.[46] As early as 1810, Rippon's *Selection* was a popular hymn book among American Baptists and later among Primitive Baptists.[47] Other influential text-only hymn books of the early nineteenth century were: *The Dover Selection* by Andrew Broaddus, published in Caroline, Virginia, in 1828; Starke Dupuy's *Hymns and Spiritual Songs, Original and Selected* published before 1818 in Kentucky; Jesse Mercer's *Cluster* from before 1810; and *The Choice* by William Dossey, published in 1830 in Philadelphia. All of the above authors eventually became associated with the pro-mission movement and therefore became less influential among Primitive Baptists after the 1830s.[48] The third edition of Mercer's *Cluster* was published in 1810 in Augusta, Georgia.

Jesse Mercer died in 1841, the year that *Primitive Hymns* was published.[49] Despite the atmosphere of intense theological discourse and partisanship, many of the sources for Benjamin Lloyd were compilations by people with whom he disagreed.[50] He did not shrink from including hymns which he thought were appropriate from these sources. In some measure, his selections may represent an acknowledgment of what Primitive Baptist congregations were singing in Alabama and Georgia at this time. *Primitive Hymns* represents not only a collection of hymns suitable for Primitive Baptists, but also a regional repertoire. For example, few hymns are shared between Lloyd's hymn book and the nation's first Primitive Baptist hymnal, *Old School Sonnets*, published in Baltimore in 1836 by James Osbourn.[51] These differences surely reflect regionalism. In the preface of *The Baptist Hymn Book* (1842) pro-mission Baptist William Buck complained about the regionality of hymn books: "Among the number there are some eight or ten that have a *local* popularity, but even *these* have defects that preclude the idea that any one of them can ever become a standard."

Sixty seven percent of the authors of the hymns in *Primitive Hymns* have been identified in researching this essay.[52] In his thesis, Don Tennyson claimed that of 68 identified authors, 59 were English and 9 were Americans. The most representative author by far was Isaac Watts. Watts was the source of 144 hymns; Phillip Doddridge authored 35; John Newton, 30; Ann Steele, 31; and Charles Wesley, 20. Other English authors such as Samuel Medley, William Cowper, John Fawcett, Benjamin Beddome, and John and Samuel Wesley were the sources of many of the other hymns. Tennyson also suggested that *Primitive Hymns* and other early American hymn books were dominated by the works of English authors due to the great influence of John Rippon's *Selection*.[53] His analysis of possible sources for *Primitive Hymns* showed that 58% of the hymns were also found in *The Dover Selection* (1828), 51% were found in the 1823 edition of Mercer's *Cluster*, and 43% were found in *The Baptist Hymnody*, a South Carolina hymnal compiled by Staunton Burdett in 1834. *Primitive Hymns* is similar to the above three early hymnals, all of which were later associated with pro-mission Baptists, in that it contains a preface, a subject index, and an index of first lines as well as hymns.[54] Tennyson points out that the main difference is the absence of overtly pro-mission hymns and the presence of certain hymns about footwashing, predestination, and election.[55] Hymns in Lloyd's hymn book relating to election and predestination include #611 and #19. Those supporting footwashing are #258-#262 and are found in the index of subjects under "Washing the Saints Feet."[56] It is interesting to note that Baptists who later supported the pro-mission movement contributed some selections, such as the missionary Baptist Adoniram Judson (#224) and the well-known Samuel Francis Smith (#219, #548, #586), author of "My country 'tis of thee." Kay Norton and others have attributed #122, #140, #167, #398, and #615 to Jesse Mercer.[57] Tunebook compiler B. F. White has been suggested as author of #515, "The glorious light of Zion." Only one of the hymns in *Primitive Hymns*, hymn #694, "My brethren dear, hear me relate," lists the author's name in a footnote at the bottom reading "this hymn was composed by Rev. F. Swint, formerly a member of the Darien Church Ga., in view of the discord produced by the introduction of the religious societies in the churches." Frederick Swint, a friend of Benjamin Lloyd, was a prominent member of Mt. Pisgah church in Stroud, Alabama, and was listed as one of the agents for *Primitive Hymns* and residing in Chambers County in 1842.[58]

Who wrote the unidentified hymns, comprising one third of the hymn book? One can only guess that at least some if not most of these authors were contemporaries of Lloyd who remain anonymous to this day. Benjamin Lloyd read and contributed to many religious periodicals of his time such as *Primitive Baptist*, *Signs of the Times*, and *The Southern Baptist Messenger*. Each of these publications featured poetry composed and contributed by the readership. Such poetry sent directly to Lloyd or read by him in such publications may have been included in *Primitive Hymns*, especially when he expanded his hymn book in its third edition (1845). However, this researcher did not find any *Primitive Hymns* texts among the poems in the *Primitive Baptist* issues from 1835 through 1845. Lloyd includes the following disclaimer in the preface of the first edition: "when there are thousands of poetical expressions from the dear followers of the Lamb since his advent into the world, in which are given their feelings from the lowest depths of sorrow and the greatest strains that ever inspired the tongue of a saint—all of which in the vicissitudes of life have been witnessed—Zion's muse may be allowed sometimes to show, that religious inspiration does not depend on critical elegance. If then there should be any thing wrong, please reject it and take the good."[59] This statement may be an apology for including the hymns of contemporaries with those of the great Watts, Doddridge, and Wesley. This disclaimer might also suggest that Lloyd himself contributed some hymns.

Primitive Hymns is coeval with the early shape note tunebooks. This may explain why so many of the tunes used to sing hymns from *Primitive Hymns* are also found in *The Sacred Harp*, *Southern Harmony*, and other similar works. Congregations associated hymns with a favorite tune that matched in meter. Tunebooks are the first documentation of these regional associations. George Pullen Jackson lists among his text sources for early shape note songs *Mercer's Cluster* (pre-1817), *Dossey's Choice*, *Rippon's Selection* (1787, 1820), various Watts collections, *Village Hymns* by Asahel Nettleton (1824), and Wyeth's *Repository of Sacred Music* (1810).[60] Many of these were sources for Benjamin Lloyd as well. Lloyd suggests tunes for only fourteen of the hymns in his hymn book. Don Tennyson believes that these tunes are named to encourage the singing of hymns that have more complicated meters such as those with a 6,6,6,6,8,8 or hallelujah meter.[61] Today, most tunes used with hymns in *Primitive Hymns* are also found in *The Sacred Harp* and *Christian Harmony*. This raises the interesting question of which came first. Do these tunebooks document tunes that the congregations were already using to sing certain hymns or have they influenced the use and popularity of certain tunes? Surely, both cases are true to an extent. There are some tunes that are used today which are not found in tunebooks and these may represent very old melodies that have escaped documentation. For example, the tune used to sing "Mercy Seat" (#333) in Bibb County, Alabama, was not included in any tunebooks until it was put in musical notation and included the *Christian Harmony* in 1958.[62]

Fifteen hundred copies of the first edition of *Primitive Hymns* were published in the summer of 1841 and advertised nationally. In *Primitive Baptist*, vol. 7, no. 8, Lloyd describes the hymn book: "The Book contains five hundred and thirty five Hymns, arranged under forty-two heads, or subjects of adaptedness to divine worship. Price for single copy, $1.00, or six copies for $5.00, in plain binding; for morocco binding and gilt, $1.50 per copy." In the same issue, he also published the preface. In 1843, the second edition was published, perhaps in another run of fifteen hundred copies. Lloyd listed a few Deep South agents and mentioned that "also, there will be a supply kept at the office of the Enquirer, Columbus, Ga. where all persons who visit Columbus can call and supply themselves." This could mean that the Columbus newspaper might have published the hymn book. Primitive Baptist Associations often paid newspapers to print their annual Minutes. These first three thousand or so copies must have made a big impact because they sold out in about two and a half years. *Primitive Hymns* gave southern Primitive Baptists a hymn book that they could call their own. In 1844, in remembrance of a deceased Elder, one of Lloyd's hymns was printed in full in an obituary in the *Primitive Baptist*. The hymn, #642, "His death we mourn, who lately stood," is attributed "From Lloyd's *Primitive Hymns*."[63] In this same year, the Beulah Association minutes state that just before adjournment, a motion was approved to "give an expression of the high regard we have of brother Benjamin Lloyd's Hymn Book, believing it to be the best we have seen; we can therefore highly recommend them to our brethren and the community in general."[64]

In a letter to *Primitive Baptist* dated August 11, 1845, Lloyd announced the new and expanded third edition with "...694 hymns, arranged under 51 general heads with a particular index of subjects, showing the subject of each hymn. The paper and type good and the binding well executed." In addition, the price for the hymn book was now: "Price in plain binding, per copy, $0.75." Furthermore he lists the "New Agents for *Primitive Hymns*" as "Eld. Gilbert Beebe, Editor of the *Signs of the Times*, is Agent for me and will supply any orders from the Northern or Middle States" and other agents from Missouri, Arkansas, Louisiana, Tennessee, and South Carolina. One might assume that Lloyd was deluged with suggestions for additional hymns during the tenure of the two editions. The third edition was printed in New York. Gilbert Beebe, perhaps the most prominent Primitive Baptist in America, may have been a major influence on *Primitive Hymns* at this stage of development. It is reasonable to assume that he helped Lloyd find his New York publisher. A larger run by a big city press would account for the lower price and the comment about its superior binding. Benjamin Lloyd arranged for Gilbert Beebe to advertise his hymnals from 1845 through 1857 in *The Signs of the Times*.

For the remainder of Lloyd's life, the hymn book changed little. There were 694 numbered hymns in the third edition, but seven doxologies are listed under #694. By 1852, these were each given a hymn number to add up to 700 but Lloyd didn't think this renumbering important enough to mention in the preface. In fact, the preface for the sixth edition was reused for the tenth (1852) and states: "There is no alteration in this from the third, and succeeding editions; as it will appear that the hymns in each bear the same numbers respectively, and the general index, and the particular index of subjects and all the references are the same in this as in previous editions since the third, which will fully illustrate its contents."[65]

By the late 1850s, there apparently was dissatisfaction among some Primitive Baptists with *Primitive Hymns*. The first strong evidence of this came in 1857 when Gilbert Beebe announced preparations for his own compilation, *The Baptist Hymn Book, comprising A Large and Choice Collection of Psalms, Hymns and Spiritual Songs, Adapted to the Faith and Order of the Old School, or Primitive Baptists, in the United States of America carefully selected from Various Authors*. This announcement appeared on the same page as advertisements for *Primitive Hymns*.[66] Beebe's hymn book was published in 1858 in Middletown, New York, by the Signs of the Times Company and was used well into the twentieth century. Circumstantial evidence might suggest that Beebe's efforts resulted from doctrinal criticism of the lyrics of some of the selections in Lloyd's hymn book. In the preface, Beebe wrote: "God's people are not justifiable in using inappropriate words, and especially such words as are untrue, in their devotional exercises; for they are admonished to sing with the UNDERSTANDING, as well as with the spirit; and so to make melody in their hearts unto the Lord. Poems have been introduced into books which are used in many congregations, that are not only destitute of the essential sentiments which the spirit of pure devotion inspires, but actually express doctrines entirely antagonistic to the doctrine of the Bible. Christians should never sing what they do not believe to be true."[67] Beebe's hymn book draws from several hymn book sources, including Lloyd's, with the author or publication attribution printed above each hymn. These attributions include: "Rippon's Col.", "Watts.," "Gadsby's Col.," and "Primitive." In time, many Primitive Baptists began using other hymn books such as Beebe's, John Clarke's *The Ebenezer Selection of Hymns and Spiritual Songs* (1856), or D. H. Goble's *Primitive Baptist Hymn Book* (1887).

Even today, some Primitive Baptists believe that *Primitive Hymns* contains "too many Arminian sentiments to be satisfactory."[68] Don Tennyson points out that some of the lyrics in Lloyd's hymn book do seem to contradict Primitive Baptist theology. Hymns that seem to support pro-mission doctrine include #142, #435, and #559.[69] This comment by one of Benjamin Lloyd's granddaughters was sent to Don Tennyson in 1972: "she could not see how her grandfather could have put some of the hymns in, as they were not sound doctrine."[70] These inconsistencies have led some to change words when singing and others to avoid certain hymns altogether, rather than give up the venerable hymn book. As Elder Donald Smith of Centreville, Alabama, states: "We received the use of the 'Primitive Hymns' by tradition from our forefathers and have never considered changing or dropping the use of it." However, some simple alterations such as replacing the word "know" to "feel" in the first verse of hymn #109 makes the hymn more acceptable. This change results in the verse: "O Jesus, my Saviour, I feel thou art mine." Some hymns such as #118, which contains a plea for sinners to choose Christ, are avoided altogether.[71]

One wonders how Benjamin Lloyd would have included hymns that would later be considered objectionable by members of his own denomination. Perhaps in 1840s all of the nuanced differences between the Primitive Baptists and Missionary Baptists had not been so fully articulated and connected to hymn texts as to divide what had been a generally agreed-upon hymnody. That scrutiny would certainly come later in the nineteenth century, and even then, the lack of a hierarchical structure among Primitive Baptists would prevent any one hymn book from being adopted by the entire denomination. Consequently, a loyal devotion to *Primitive Hymns* was maintained by many communities and continues to this day.

These faithful groups of patrons were served by successive generations of the Lloyd family, especially Naomi Lloyd. Naomi A. Lloyd and her son Benjamin were named executors of Benjamin Lloyd's estate in 1858. There is no evidence that the book was printed during the Civil War years. However, Naomi, with the help of her children, kept the hymn book in print throughout Reconstruction. She continued using the 1858 preface that Benjamin wrote after moving to Butler County. Naomi Ann Lloyd married Peter Cheatham (1812-1867), probably during the war years. Perhaps in deference to her late husband and because she remarried, the title page on editions during these years remained unchanged listing "Benjamin Lloyd, Minister of the Gospel, Greenville," as proprietor.[72]

Naomi Lloyd Cheatham provided the critical link for the hymn books' survival. Since her marriage to Benjamin Lloyd in 1832, she bore from eighteen to twenty-one babies. Of these, fourteen lived to adulthood. Raising these children, with a husband who was often away preaching, must have been an exhausting experience. And yet, after her husbands death, in the midst of the Civil War and after remarriage, she still had the strength to tend her children's hymn book legacy left to them by their father. During these lean years, few, if any changes were made to the book. In fact, nicks and cuts in the lead type used again and again to print the hymn book produced blemishes in succeeding editions (see Editions Appendix). When she died on August 7, 1884, she had overseen production of *Primitive Hymns* for a quarter of a century. Naomi was buried next to her first husband in the small Lloyd family cemetery at "the Palings" in Fort Dale.

Of all their children, Jesse Cox Lloyd, the tenth son of Benjamin and Naomi Lloyd, must have been the most interested in the publication of *Primitive Hymns*.[73] He is listed as proprietor in the 1890 and 1893 editions, both published in Butler Springs, even though he had moved his family to Montgomery in 1890. There are not many copies of J.C. Lloyd's edition of the hymn book, and he apparently made few or no changes. When he died in 1892, his wife Martha ("Mattie") Eliza Reynolds Lloyd (1853-1919) must have overseen the publication of the 1893 edition, keeping his name as proprietor.

In 1895, Mattie Lloyd remarried. Soon thereafter, her second husband A. V. Atkins, a Primitive Baptist elder, moved the family to Temple, Texas.[74] In Temple, she presided over publication of editions in 1897, 1900, and 1906. It was in this period that *Primitive Hymns* underwent its most significant alterations since the third edition. Apparently, Mrs. Atkins chose to remove the hymn, "The Romish Lady." This alteration did not last long. The hymn is not in the 1900 edition, but was put back in within a few years. The following preface is from the edition published in 1906:

> I wish to add to the above [the 1858 preface] that on the death of my dear mother [Mrs. Benjamin Lloyd] who requested her son [J. C. Lloyd] my former husband, to purchase the type and business from the estate of his father [Elder Benjamin Lloyd] and keep up the publication of the Book, which he did as long as his life was spared, since his death it has been my great and conscientious desire to make the Book without fault as far as possible. I have enlarged the type which makes it now clear and suitable for the aged, as well as the young. I have added five hymns and reinstated the hymn titled 'The Romish Lady.' My humble prayer to God has been that he would sustain me in all my efforts to keep this Book in its purity. With deepest gratitude to all my friends and patrons I am your humble servant in God.
>
> Mrs. M. E. Atkins
> Temple, Texas.

The hymn book now had 705 hymns and it is this edition that is printed in facsimile today. The five hymns in this edition that are not in the 1845 enlarged third edition are: #687, “Rock of ages,” by Augustus Toplady; #688, “We shall sleep, but not forever,” by an unknown author; #689, “Land of rest,” by Elizabeth Mills; #690, “The Lord is my Shepherd” (Twenty-third Psalm), by James Montgomery; and #691, “Oh, to be robed and ready,” by an unknown author. “Land of Rest” appears in the “Index of First Lines” indexed both by its first line, “O land of rest for thee I sigh,” and its title. This might suggest that it was also dropped from an earlier edition and then added back.

The modifications of the hymn book were a source of disappointment to some Primitive Baptists who had grown to love the old 1845 enlarged edition’s selection of 700 hymns. This change may have prompted some to stop using the book. At some point, Mrs. Atkins or her daughters began publishing both the 700 and 705 hymn versions of the book to satisfy the needs of their patrons. Editions of the hymn book from 1946 and 1963 containing 700 hymns can be found amongst the Alabaha River Primitive Baptist Association of south Georgia and they may have been the primary reason why the 700 hymn edition was kept in print. Their preference for the 700 hymn addition was in part to keep the numbering of hymns the same, a considerable concern since hymns are referred to by number. Also, some believed that the “Romish Lady” was not in the 705 version. This hymn is in the modern 705 version. In the 1906 edition, Mrs. Atkins stated in her Preface that she was reinstating the hymn, but somehow the hymn was still left out. When the hymn was reinstated in the 1921 edition, the listing of the hymn in the back may have continued the confusion. After the reinstatement, it appears in the first-lines index as “The Romish Lady,” its title, and not by its first line, “There was a Romish lady, brought up in popery” (as it had appeared until at least 1893). In 1975, after the copyright changed hands, the Alabaha Association had to arrange a special printing of the 700 hymn edition with the new publishers, the Primitive Hymns Corporation. By ordering the hymn book in its 700 hymn version, this South Georgia community made sure that they and their neighbors had the book as Benjamin Lloyd intended it to be. The 700 hymn version contents are the same as the *Primitive Hymns* editions from 1845 until 1893.

“The Romish Lady” was a well known ballad that appeared in broadsides during the early nineteenth century.[75] The piece was not among those included by Beebe in his 1858 hymn book. But the hymn was included, in the early twentieth century, by Elder C. H. Cayce in *The Good Old Songs Hymn Book*. The reason why Mrs. Atkins would remove this hymn from *Primitive Hymns* has intrigued both singers and scholars. At the time of its removal, either 1897 or 1900, there was considerable anti-Catholic sentiment in the United States. This was due to the influx of Catholic immigrants from southern and eastern Europe. Perhaps, in her effort to “make the Book without fault as far as possible,” Mrs. Atkins did not want the hymn book associated with this wave of xenophobia. The reinstatement of the hymn was most certainly the result of comments and requests from her many patrons. Comments from a gathering of singers at Bethel Church in Berlin, Alabama, in 1998 suggest “The Romish Lady” was once a popular hymn but many congregations do not sing it due to its overt criticism of Catholicism. This congregation as well as members of the Lee family of south Georgia said that they believe that the text is based on a true story. Elder Donald Smith of Centreville states that "Romish Lady" is not considered controversial in his community, but it is not sung very often.[76] Judging from comments of contemporary singers, the hymn could be interpreted as a group memory of the persecution of Anglican dissenters in early America and can be seen as critical of both Anglican and Catholic doctrine, a comparison the English Puritans certainly made.

The longest hiatus in publishing *Primitive Hymns* may have been from 1906 until 1921. No editions, in either public or private hands, have been found for these years. During this tumultuous period the family moved, a world war was fought, Mrs. M. E. (Mattie) Atkins died (1919), and the daughters married. According to a letter written by La Verte Lloyd Smith and sent to Oliver Weaver, A. V. and Mattie Atkins moved to California in 1910 where daughters Opal and La Verte found husbands. Opal married Homer Terry and La Verte married Preston Smith in California. The sisters bought the "hymn book business" from their mother's estate by sealed bid.[77] In 1921, Opal Lloyd Terry and La Verte Lloyd Smith renewed publication and added a short addendum after their grandfather's 1858 preface. It reads:

> Since the death of our dear mother [Mrs. M. E. Atkins], who so earnestly requested that the publication of the Book be kept up and in the family, we wish to say that we have purchased the copyright, stereotype plates, all the claims and everything pertaining to the business from her estate and will continue the publication of the Book under the same style and standard, and it is our sincere desire to give prompt attention to all orders.
>
> Opal Lloyd Terry
> La Verte Lloyd Smith, Manager
> February 4, 1921
> La Mesa, California

This statement was included in each of the editions until 1971 (the special 700-hymn edition still carries this addendum). It was probably in the 1935 printing that this statement, "Entered according to act of Congress in the year 1934, by Opal Lloyd Terry and La Verte Lloyd Smith," appeared. With the copyright renewed, the women continued publishing the hymn book and selling it to a faithful constituency. Until about 1937, La Verte Smith ran the small company and then her sister Opal took over for the next thirty years. Opal Terry died in 1967 and La Verte once again took over the publishing duties.[78] During the last years of La Verte Smith's management of *Primitive Hymns*, sales continued to be brisk, by her estimation. The book was reprinted on average every two or three years, with sales of 1,663 books in 1967 and 1,541 in 1968. In 1969, at the time of her letter to Oliver Weaver, La Verte Smith was childless and the heirs of her sister's estate did not want to manage the hymn book company. It is no wonder that she fretted over the future of her grandfather's hymn book. In referring to her patrons, she wrote: "I haven't informed these dear Primitive Baptists I am going on 84, and I won't, but who knows *who* will take over in my place...."[79] She did, however, inform some of her patrons of her dilemma, for in 1971, a group of Primitive Baptists from eastern North Carolina bought the hymn book business from her.

In 1971, the copyright to *Primitive Hymns* was sold to the Primitive Hymns Corporation of Rocky Mount, North Carolina. This corporation was formed to "keep Benjamin Lloyd's hymn book in print" after a member of the Contentnea Association of eastern North Carolina found out that La Verte Smith had broken her hip and could not continue publishing.[80] Others from the Contentnea Association, along with some members of the Black Creek, Kehukee, and Seven Miles Associations formed a company of nineteen stockholders. In 1972, a year after this transition, La Verte Smith told Don Tennyson that the new publishers "will carry on as long as there is a demand for this hymn book and I believe that there always will be Old Line Primitive Baptists who will not have any other hymn book."[81] Since 1971, the Primitive Hymns Corporation has provided hymn books to singers in thirty states.[82] Seven years later, in 1978, La Verte Lloyd Smith died.

Primitive Hymns Today

For the last 160 years, there has been a relationship between metered hymn singing and shape note singing in the South. Primitive Baptists have participated in shape note singing since at least the 1830s and they are the mainstay of that tradition today. The widespread revival of shape note singing has brought northern and western singers in contact with southern Primitive Baptists who also sing from Lloyd's hymn book. Many have been drawn to southern singers such as Donald Smith of Centreville, Alabama, Don Clark of Lafayette, Alabama, and the Lee family of Hoboken, Georgia, who have been outspoken in their affection for *Primitive Hymns*. When pressed, Clarke and David Lee admit that they have fostered an interest in Lloyd's book among those who have not grown up with it. For this reason, selections from Lloyd's are often sung informally before or after more highly structured Sacred Harp singings as far away as Chicago.

Even among many Primitive Baptists there is a realization that singing styles are changing. In 1988, Paul Drummond suggested that the "lining out" of hymns had almost died out.[83] In south Georgia, the most conservative Primitive Baptists like to line out hymns as a conscious link to past practices.[84] It is a practice that most churches wanted to show this researcher, but sometimes the groups had trouble finding someone who was comfortable lining a hymn. To those concerned with preserving their traditions, *Primitive Hymns* represents the old way of singing. When faced with the extinction of *Primitive Hymns*, a group of North Carolina Primitive Baptists bought the rights from La Verte Smith "out of love" for Benjamin Lloyd's book. They did not want the hymn book they grew up with to go out of print.[85]

There is no doubt that Elder Lloyd's hymn book is much appreciated today in a variety of contexts, but the most important one remains the meeting house. Don Clark of Lafayette, Alabama, speaks for many when he points out that the appreciation of metered hymn singing or Sacred Harp singing as simply an old folk art tradition is missing the point. These hymns and traditions have been propagated not by academic, artistic, or educational interests, but though the religious faith of thousands of believers for many generations. Elder Donald Smith speaks eloquently about the spiritual aspect of singing: "Sometimes the feeling or 'spirit' we feel while singing from the 'hymn book' is beyond expression and we, most of the time, do not even ask which book is that tune in, etc. [It] doesn't matter, the hymn book has no 'tunes.' We usually...refer to 'raising a hymn' in the hymn book and sometimes we have felt the Spirit as much in the tune selected or raised as we have in the singing of the hymn itself. This is hard to explain, but I will say this; some of the hymns at times are special because, at the moment, the tune fits the sentiments of the poetry in it."[86] One thing that an article like this can never do is capture the sincerity, love, and spirituality expressed through singing out of Lloyd's *Primitive Hymns*. That can only be experienced firsthand.

Notes

1 Selma L. Bishop, *Isaac Watts: Hymns and Spiritual Songs, 1707-1748* (London: The Faith Press, 1962), xvii.

2 Bishop, xvi.

3 Louis F. Benson, *The English Hymn: Its Development and Use in Worship* (1915; reprint, Richmond: John Knox Press, 1962), 143.

4 R. Paul Drummond, *A Portion for the Singers: A History of Music Among Primitive Baptists since 1800* (Atwood, Tennessee: The Christian Baptist Library and Publishing Co., Inc., 1988), 39.

5 Christine Leigh Heyrman, *Southern Cross: The Beginnings of the Bible Belt* (New York: Knopf, 1997), 10, 15-17.

6 John Gordon Crowley, *The Primitive Baptists of South Georgia and Florida* (Doctoral dissertation, Florida State University, 1996), 24; Heyrman, 20-21.

7 Crowley, 6-8, 24.

8 Crowley, 13-14.

9 Don Tennyson, *A Study of Benjamin Lloyd's "The Primitive Hymns"* (Master of Church Music thesis, New Orleans Theological Seminary, 1973), 9.

10 Crowley, 34.

11 Tennyson, 5-7.

12 Drummond, 70-71.

13 Drummond, 21.

14 John Leland, "Virginia Chronicle" (1790) in *The Writings of Elder John Leland, Including Some Events of His Life. Written by Himself, With Additional Sketches*, ed. L. F. Greene (New York: G. W. Wood, 1845; reprint, New York: Arno Press and the New York Times, 1969), 115.

15 John Rippon, *A Selection of Hymns from the Best Authors Intended to be an Appendix to Dr. Watts' Psalms and Hymns* (New York: William Durrell, 1792), xi, xii.

16 William J. Cooper and Thomas E. Terrill, *The American South: A History* (New York: Knopf, 1990), 260.

17 Crowley, 29.

18 Crowley, 308.

19 Harry L. Eskew, "Use and Influence of Hymnals in Southern Baptist Churches up to 1915," in *Singing Baptists: Studies in Baptist Hymnody in America* (Nashville: Church Street Press, 1994), 182.

20 Drummond, 22, 30.

21 Wayne Flynt, *Alabama Baptists: Southern Baptists in the Heart of Dixie* (Tuscaloosa: University of Alabama Press, 1998), 11.

22 C. Ray Brewster, The Cluster *of Jesse Mercer* (Macon, Georgia: Renaissance Press, 1983), 7.

23 Oliver C. Weaver, "Benjamin Lloyd: A Pioneer Baptist in Alabama" *Alabama Review* 21 (April 1968): 146.

24 Weaver, 147.

25 Bobby L. Lindsey, *"The Reason for the Tears": A History of Chambers County, Alabama* (West Point, Georgia: Hester Printing Company, Chattahoochee Valley Historical Society, 1971), 284.

[26] Weaver, 148.
[27] Chambers County Will Book.
[28] Chambers County Marriage License, vol. 1, p. 152.
[29] Crowley, 104.
[30] Lindsey, 284; Weaver, 148-149.
[31] Weaver, 150.
[32] Hosea Holcombe, *A History of the Rise and Progress of the Baptists in Alabama: With a Miniature History of the Denomination from the Apostolic Age Down to the Present Time, Interpreted with Anecdotes Original and Selected, and Concluded with an Address to the Baptists of Alabama* (Philadelphia: King and Baird, Printers, 1840), 267.
[33] Holcombe, 294-295.
[34] Flynt, 33.
[35] Crowley, 170.
[36] Benjamin Lloyd, letter to the editor, *Primitive Baptist* 6 (March 18, 1841): 92.
[37] Benjamin Lloyd, letter to the editor, *Primitive Baptist* 6 (July 12, 1841): 226.
[38] Weaver, 151.
[39] Benjamin Lloyd, letter to the editor, *Primitive Baptist* 8 (December 30, 1843): 31.
[40] Weaver, 151.
[41] Weaver, 152.
[42] George Evans Brewer, "History of Coosa County," *Alabama Historical Quarterly* 4 (1942): 81.
[43] Tennyson, 19-20.
[44] Benjamin Lloyd, letter to the editor, *Primitive Baptist* 6 (March 18, 1841): 92.
[45] John Bealle, *Public Worship, Private Faith: Sacred Harp and American Folksong* (Athens: University of Georgia Press, 1997), 11-16, 154-59.
[46] William Jensen Reynolds, *Hymns of Our Faith* (Nashville: Broadman Press, 1967), xvii.
[47] Drummond, 60.
[48] Drummond, 63-64.
[49] Brewster, 6.
[50] Despite many modern observations about how some selections from *Primitive Hymns* are doctrinally unsound, the hymn book was wildly popular in its early years. It was not until the late 1850s when one sees evidence of dissatisfaction in some quarters.
[51] Tennyson, 33.
[52] In his 1972 masters thesis, Don Tennyson indicated that he had identified 52% of the authors of the hymns in *Primitive Hymns*, but did not provide a table attributing particular hymns to particular authors. This writer has identified 67%, but has no way of knowing how many were also identified by Tennyson.
[53] Tennyson, 25.
[54] Tennyson, 26.
[55] Tennyson, 28.
[56] Tennyson, 30-31.
[57] Kay Norton, electronic mail message to the author, February 20, 1999.
[58] Benjamin Lloyd, letters to the editor, *Primitive Baptist* 7 (April 7, 1842), 119.
[59] Ibid., 120.
[60] George Pullen Jackson, *White Spirituals in the Southern Uplands* (Chapel Hill: University of North Carolina Press, 1933), 154-155.
[61] Tennyson, 32.
[62] Donald Smith, letter to the author, February 24, 1999. Elder Smith identified the following as other hymns that are sung to tunes not found in tunebooks: #2, #109, #206, #258, #362, #382, #533, #632, and #691.
[63] Luke Haynie, letter to the editor, *Primitive Baptist* 9 (1844): 12.
[64] Beulah Baptist Association, Minutes of the Seventh Annual Session (1844), 3. On

microfilm at Samford University, Birmingham, Alabama.

[65] Benjamin Lloyd, preface, *Primitive Hymns*, 1852 edition.

[66] Gilbert Beebe, "Proposals for a New Hymn Book," *Southern Baptist Messenger* 7 (1857): 88.

[67] Gilbert Beebe, preface, *The Baptist Hymn Book, comprising A Large and Choice Collection of Psalms, Hymns and Spiritual Songs, Adapted to the Faith and Order of the Old School, or Primitive Baptists, in the United States of America carefully selected from Various Authors*, 5th ed. (Middletown, N.Y.: Signs of the Times, 1877).

[68] Beverly Bush Patterson, *The Sound of the Dove: Singing in Appalachian Primitive Baptist Churches* (Urbana: University of Illinois Press, 1995), 43.

[69] Tennyson, 29-30.

[70] Tennyson, 29.

[71] Donald Smith, letter to the author.

[72] According to Oliver Weaver, Naomi Cheatham insisted that her grandchildren call her "grandmother Lloyd," not "grandmother Cheatham."

[73] La Verte Lloyd Smith, letter to Oliver Weaver, June 22, 1969. Mrs. Smith states her belief that her father's (Jesse Cox Lloyd) inheritance from his mother (Naomi Lloyd Cheatham) was the rights to the hymn book.

[74] In a list of "Agents for the Primitive Pathway," in 1877, A. V. Atkins is listed as living in Belton, Texas. So, Mr. Atkins came to Alabama for some reason, married the widow Lloyd, and returned to Texas with his new family. See *The Primitive Pathway* 2 (September 1, 1877).

[75] "The Romish Lady" is a story of a young woman who rejects the idolatry of her Catholic upbringing and consequently is burned at the stake. Some lines from the text appear in a British play from the early seventeenth century. The version more similar to that in *Primitive Hymns* was printed on many broadsides in the United States during the nineteenth century. It is indexed as #Q32 in Malcolm G. Laws, *American Balladry From British Broadsides* (Philadelphia: University of Pennsylvania, 1957), 288. The song was also known as a ballad in Alabama and included in Byron Arnold, *Folksongs of Alabama* (Tuscaloosa: University of Alabama Press, 1950), 19. A 1937 field recording of it can be heard on Yazoo CD 2014, *The Music of Kentucky,* Vol. 2.

[76] Donald Smith, letter to the author.

[77] La Verte Lloyd Smith, letter to Oliver Weaver.

[78] In her letter to Oliver Weaver, Mrs. Smith states that she took over the publication in 1967, even though Opal Terry's granddaughters owned, at different times, one-fourth or one-half of the company.

[79] La Verte Lloyd Smith, letter to Oliver Weaver.

[80] Bettie Woodard, telephone conversation with the author, March 2, 1999.

[81] Tennyson, 35.

[82] According to Bettie Woodard of the Primitive Hymns Corporation, the great majority of sales are to southern states. The entire list of states include: Alabama, Arizona, Arkansas, California, Delaware, the District of Columbia, Florida, Georgia, Illinois, Indiana, Kansas, Kentucky, Louisiana, Maine, Maryland, Michigan, Mississippi, Missouri, New Jersey, New York, North Carolina, Ohio, Oklahoma, Pennsylvania, South Carolina, Tennessee, Texas, Virginia, Washington, and West Virginia. By contrast, in 1972, Tennyson's survey showed that the book was being used in "most southern states; Michigan, Ohio, Pennsylvania, Washington, D. C., New York, and Oregon."

[83] Drummond, 21.

[84] Crowley, 28.

[85] Bettie Woodard, telephone conversation with the author.

[86] Donald Smith, letter to the author.

THE PRIMITIVE HYMNS:
DESCRIPTIONS OF EXTANT EDITIONS

COMPILED BY JOEY BRACKNER

The following descriptions of the editions of *The primitive hymns, spiritual songs, and sacred poems: regularly selected, classified and set in order, and adapted to social singing and all occasions of divine worship* by Benjamin Lloyd was compiled by Joey Brackner during research for his article in this book. Examination of these editions gave some insight into the evolution of the book through the years. These copies were found in both public and private holdings, so the location (or citation) of those examined or acknowledged are in parentheses. Each of the prefaces are printed in full with the description of the edition in which that preface first appears. It is almost certain that there are a few editions that exist but escaped this search.

The many subtle changes to the hymn book through time help tell its story. Elder Lloyd stopped numbering his editions after the tenth because he stopped revising the hymn selections, so each succeeding edition was identical. For this reason, the "proprietors" of the hymn book used the same printing plates from the early 1850's, when the hymns were renumbered to a total of 700, through 1897 or 1900, when the first enlarged print edition appeared. We know this because damage to the printing plates resulted in certain imperfections, such as the "6" on hymn 651, which became less and less visible in succeeding editions. In the last few editions of the nineteenth century the "6" on hymn 651 cannot be seen. The hymn book was originally 12-13 centimeters in height. When Mrs. Atkins revised it, in 1897 or 1900, she also enlarged the book to its present height of 15-16 centimeters. A casual observer looking at different editions from the midnineteenth century might argue that the book changed greatly. For example, the 1852 and 1869 editions both have 558 pages and identical contents, but because the rag content of the pages in the 1869 hymn book is much lower, the book is much thinner. All editions of the hymn book contain this quotation from Isaiah on the title page: "And the ransomed of the Lord shall return and come to Zion with songs and everlasting joys; they shall obtain gladness, and sorrow and sighing shall flee away." In the modern (post 1921) editions, the "Index of Subjects" remains keyed to the earlier edition of 700 hymns, for example, the "Advent of Christ" hymns are listed as 20-32, and should be 20-30. The 1858 preface, the last written by Elder Lloyd, has appeared in every edition since 1858. The deletion and reintroduction of "The Romish Lady" by Mrs. M. E. Atkins is dealt with elsewhere in this book. Suffice it to say, this attempted change has caused some confusion to some patrons of the hymn book through the years. This hymn is in the modern editions.

The Editions:

1841, first edition. A letter dated April 7, 1842 and published in the April 23 edition of the *Primitive Baptist* states: "The Book contains five hundred and thirty five Hymns, arranged under forty-two heads, or subjects of adaptedness to divine worship. Price for single copy, $1.00, or six copies for $5.00, in plain binding; for morocco binding and gilt, $1.50 per copy." A letter written July 12, 1841, and published in the August 14 edition of the *Primitive Baptist* stated that 1500 copies would be available to the public on August 15, 1841. Although no known copy of this hymnal exists, Lloyd offered his "prefatory remarks for the satisfaction of all who feel interested" in the *Primitive Baptist*, vol. 7, no. 8 (Sat., April 23, 1842), pp. 119-120:

> Dear Brethren and Sisters in the Lord: I now present to you and the public in general, this volume of Hymns and Spiritual songs and to the doing of which, I choose either to give you a statement of relative circumstances, than to offer you an apology for the work. Having become impressed with a sense of the importance of a well adapted Hymn Book among the Primitive Baptists at this time, and having been solicited to publish such a one; sensible of my incapacity for a work of so much importance, unaided by the spirit of God, deeply affected with a love for the truth, for the cause of God, and a peculiar regard for his dear children on earth; I endeavored to seek the direction of that God who cannot err, and who is a sun and shield to his people, and who alone is able to bless all our labors, and who will lead us in the paths of duty. Then under the strongest impressions of my duty, of the utility and of the actual demand of the church of Jesus Christ, (which I hope we are), relying on the faithful hand of God to sustain me, the liberality of the brethren and generosity of the public, I was induced to undertake so formidable a task; hoping that the work might be so rendered and so suited to the various occasions of worship, and its style such as to recommend itself in such manner as to secure circulation, and that degree of patronage which I humbly hope I am justly entitled to.
>
> As such, I have been disposed to follow the impressions of my mind, and leave the event with God. At the same time humbly praying his blessing upon my effort to promote his cause, to glorify his name, and to give success to my desire that the hearts of his dear ransomed ones may often be cheered by singing the songs of Zion, and that he
>
> Will smile on each divine attempt
> To spread the gospel rays.
>
> In this book, I have arranged the Hymns and spiritual Songs under different heads, or classes. And have pursued that order which appeared to me to agree with the plan of salvation, and the effect and progress of the gospel and the teachings of the Holy Spirit, by which the dear children of God are brought to a knowledge of the truth, and led to the ordinances of the gospel, and enabled to walk in them to the glory of their

heavenly Father. "And all thy children shall be taught of the Lord, and great shall be the peace of thy children."

The Hymns of the various subjects and the ordinances of the gospel, as they stand in order are so arranged that the minister, or lay member need only to know the subject upon which he wishes to sing, and by a glance at the index of subjects he can be immediately directed to an appropriate Hymn.

With regard to the spirit and sentiment of the various Hymns contained in this work, I have labored to introduce only such as appear to me to correspond with the word of God, the gospel, the voice of inspiration, and the ordinances. Should any thing appear to the contrary, I trust I shall have the lenity of my brethren; for I do assure them if this should be the case, it is not by design, but is either attributable to an oversight, or a want of competency to judge correctly. Also, brethren, let it be remembered, that in so formidable a work, when there are thousands of poetical expressions from the dear followers of the Lamb since his advent into the world, in which are given their feelings from the lowest depths of sorrow and the greatest strains that ever inspired the tongue of a saint—all of which in the vicissitudes of life have been witnessed—Zion's muse may be allowed sometimes to show, that religious inspiration does not depend on critical elegance. If then there should be any thing wrong, please reject it and take the good. And while I may address you, my feelings are stated, and my head is inspired with the blessed hope, that I shall see many of you in the flesh. And while I am going to and fro to preach salvation through Jesus Christ, though I am consumed by the drought of summer and the frost of winter, as many of my preaching brethren are, I yet hope we shall sing the praises of God together, and tell of redeeming grace and dying love, if not in time, in eternity. And in conclusion, I feel conscious that I now present to my brethren and the community in general, as good and as well adapted Hymn Book as could reasonably have been expected; whether it be the best yet extant, is left to others to determine. I pray the sanctifying influence of the Spirit of God to attend it, and all his dear children.

With sentiments of the highest Christian regard and esteem, I submit myself in the bonds of the gospel; your humble obedient servant, &c. Benjamin Lloyd.

(no extant copy)

1843-44, second edition. It was probably identical to the first edition and most likely published in 1844. (No extant copy)

1845, third edition. "Corrected and Enlarged." This is the most important of all editions. It was this version of the hymn book that remained unchanged almost to the end of the nineteenth century.

PREFACE, To Ministers, Churches, and Others: In presenting the third edition of my Hymn Book to the public, it becomes my duty to give the reasons why it appears so soon after the publication of the second, and also to account for the slight alterations which have been made. The second edition all being brought into use, the third has been called for. I have, therefore, given it a critical and patient review; and in doing this, I have made such alterations as I consider important to be made; and I hope the improvement derived from such alterations will be as acceptable to its friends as they are satisfactory for the labor they have cost me.

From the arrangement of the general index of subjects, the distribution of the additional hymns under their appropriate heads will prevent an agreement in the numbers of the hymns in the second and third editions, and, owing to the alterations in some of the hymns, I have thought best not to give a reference in the new book to the number of the hymns in the old one; and I thought it better to distribute the additional hymns under their appropriate heads than to embody them in an appendix, and the more so as I had to introduce three new heads in the general index of subjects.

From a sense of my obligation to God, and a sense of duty to the Church, as well as a sense of gratitude to the brethren for the great interest they have taken for me in the distribution of my hymn book, and the extensive circulation and general use of it in the churches, I was deeply impressed with the imperious duty of rendering it as useful and as valuable as it was possible for me to do, and in the mean time to try to employ the liberal patronage of the brethren and friends of the work in improving it, and also to put it at a less price than the former editions. I hope, therefore, that no person will think that I have introduced the third edition with its improvements, differing from the second, in order that the second may be laid aside and the brethren be compelled to purchase the third; but as the second edition was all in use, and as I had to offer the third, I thought it would be no objection to offer it with its improvements; I have, therefore, carefully revised the whole work, and the alterations have been made in the forms of expression where it was necessary, in order better to adapt the hymns to be sung; and some verses have been left out, but in no case to alter the spirit of the hymn, but to improve it. The changes are mainly to improve the expression, and to afford more ease in singing; the omission of verses is either where the hymns were objectionable on account of their length, or rendered more useful thereby, and no injury done to the sentiment. An effort has been made to arrange the hymns agreeably to the natural order of mental association and of Christian experience; so that a person acquainted with evangelical truth and religious emotions, will find in his own bosom an Index to the successive subjects. It is hoped that hymns will be found in this book adapted to every important subject on which a minister of Christ would be likely to address a congregation.

In proportion to the interesting and various content of any volume must be the necessity of suitable reference. A copious index gives facility of use to every important publication, and therefore it must be indispensably necessary in such hymn books as are used constantly in public worship, and by many Christian families every day in the year. I have, therefore, published this third edition with a particular index of subjects, which shows the subject of each hymn contained in the work. I have exerted all the ability I have in the effort to furnish the brethren and churches with a hymn book embracing hymns suited to all occasions of worship, with the easiest possible method of selection; and in doing this, I have been deeply conscious of my responsibility.

The work is dedicated to Christ and the Church. If it shall tend to the elevation of evangelical taste, the interest of worship, and the glory of God, my aims will be accomplished. To his peculiar blessing, to the candor of my brethren in the ministry, and to the patronage of my fellow Christians and a generous public, I humbly commit the work; and remain, with high considerations of Christian love and esteem,

Their brother and servant in the Gospel,

Benjamin Lloyd
Wetumpka, Ala, January 16, 1845

(Special Collections, Gorgas Library, University of Alabama)

1846, fourth edition. "Fourth Edition Published for the Proprietor, and for sale by him at Wetumpka, Al. 1846." The fourth edition is identical to the third edition. (Christian Baptist Library, Atwood, Tennessee)

1849, fifth edition. (An advertisement in the May 12, 1849 edition of the *Primitive Baptist* announces the availability of the fifth edition of *Primitive Hymns*. Lloyd dates the advertisement March 12, 1849.)

Late 1849 or 1850, sixth edition. (The sixth edition is mentioned in the preface of the 1852, tenth edition where he comments that the third through the sixth editions are exactly the same. One might assume by his reuse of the preface of the sixth edition that the third through the tenth edition might also be identical.)

1852, tenth edition. "Tenth Edition Published for the prop. and for sale by him at Wetumpka." The preface reads:

To Ministers, Churches and Others; I now present the tenth edition of my Hymn book to the public and in doing so I only deem it necessary to repeat what I have said in a former edition, as fully expressive of all that is required to be said in this; there being so many renewed expressions from the brethren of their approval of the present method of arrangement. There is no alteration in this from the third, and succeeding editions; as it will appear that the hymns in each bear the same numbers respectively, and the general index, and the particular index of subjects and all the references are the same in this as in previous editions since the third, which will fully illustrate its contents.

In view of the divine favor conferred upon me in enabling me to prepare a Hymn book which has so fully met the views of the brethren and Churches, and given such general satisfaction, and obtained so extensive a circulation in so short a time, that the seventh edition is already called for. I could not write this preface without manifesting a renewed sense of gratitude to God and obligation to the brethren for their very kind and Christian expressions to me, and the great interest they have been pleased to take for my success. With such emotions as must abide in my heart in reviewing these expressions, and the very favorable reception of my book, I cannot forbear to express with humble gratitude the great desire I have that all the praise may be ascribed to the God of all grace, the Father, the Son and the Holy Ghost, and that my humble efforts through this medium may be sanctified to very many of the followers of our Divine Master. To his peculiar blessing, the favorable consideration of my brethren, and the patronage of a generous public, I humbly commit this seventh edition also. With my best desires for their spiritual and temporal welfare, I remain their brother and Servant in the Gospel, etc.

Benjamin Lloyd
Wetumpka, Ala, August 1, 1851

(anonymous owner)

1858 edition. Published in Greenville, Alabama. The preface reads:

To MINISTERS, CHURCHES AND OTHERS.

The present method of arrangement of this book has been highly approved by a great many Ministers and other brethren, and many of them have given the kindest expressions for its success and extensive circulation. Its general use and circulation have increased more and more; and the higher estimate is placed upon the work by those who are best acquainted with its contents. Its easy method of arrangement, the general index and particular index, so fully illustrate its rich variety of subjects, that persons can easily select hymns suited to any occasion of Divine Service.

In view of the Divine favor conferred on me in enabling me to prepare a Hymn Book which has so fully met the views of the brethren and churches, and given such general satisfaction I can but give a renewed expression of my sense of gratitude to God, and obligations to the brethren for their many kind and Christian expressions to me and the great interest they have been pleased to take for my success.

With such emotions as must abide in my heart in reviewing those expressions, and the very favorable reception of my book, I cannot forbear to express with humble gratitude the great desire I have that all the praise may be ascribed to the God of all grace, the Father, the Son, and the Holy Ghost, and that my humble efforts through this medium may be sanctified to very many of the dear followers of our Divine Master.

To His peculiar blessing , the favorable consideration of my brethren, and the patronage of a generous public, the work is humbly committed.

With my best desires for their spiritual and temporal welfare,

I remain their brother and
Servant in the Gospel, &c.,
BENJAMIN LLOYD
Greenville, Ala., July 8, 1858.

(Appalachian State University, University of North Carolina)

1869 edition. Published in Greenville. (Anonymous owner)

1870 edition. Published in Greenville. (Special Collections, Gorgas Library, University of Alabama)

1872 edition. (Alabama Department of Archives and History; Samford University; Birmingham Public Library)

1876 edition. Published in Greenville. (Samford University)

1877 edition. Published in Greenville. (Southwestern Baptist Theological Seminary Library, Fort Worth, Texas)

1880 edition. Published in Greenville. (Samford University)

1882 edition. Published in Greenville. (Virginia Technological Seminary)

1887 edition. Published in Greenville. (Samford University)

1890 edition. Published in "Butler Springs, Ala.,...for the Proprietor, J. C. Lloyd." Hymn #687 is "The Romish Lady." (Emory University)

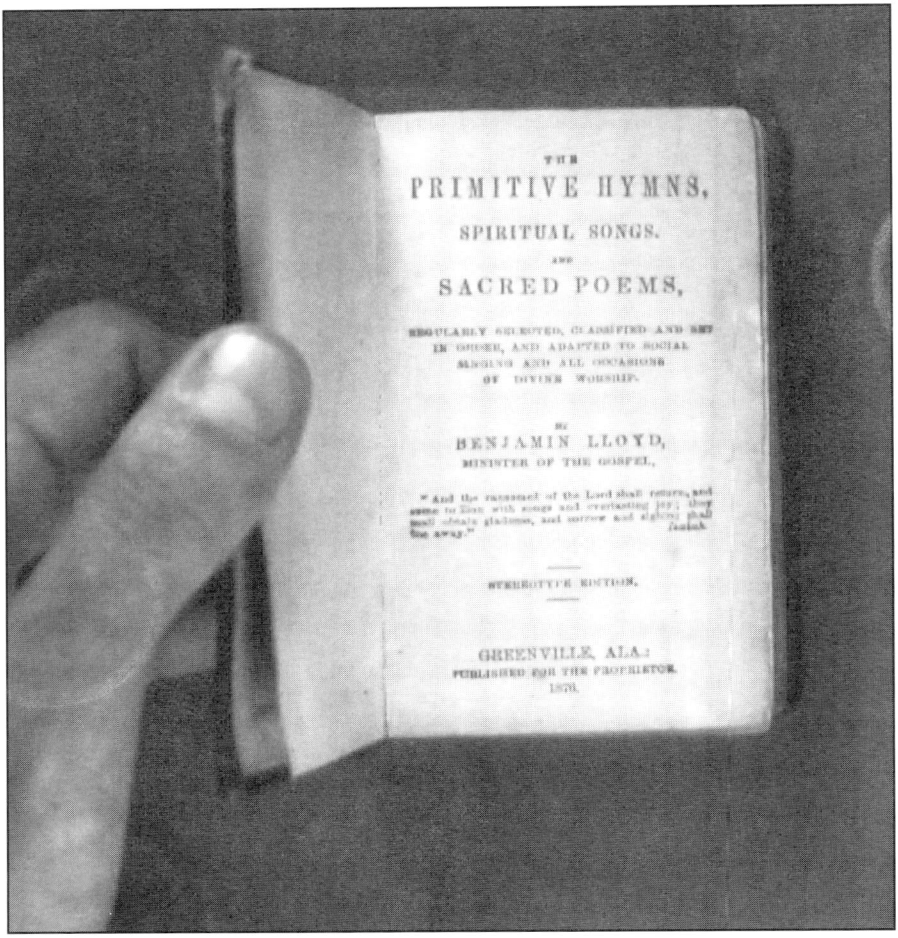

Joey Brackner

This 1876 edition of The Primitive Hymns has a brown leather cover with gold tooling and gilt-edged pages and is 13 cm. in height.

1891 edition. (Cited in Don Tennyson, *A Study of Benjamin Lloyd's "The Primitive Hymns"* [Master of Church Music thesis, New Orleans Theological Seminary, 1973], plate II, p. 27.)

1893 edition. Published in "Butler Springs, Ala.,...for the Proprietor, J. C. Lloyd." Hymn #687 is "The Romish Lady." (University of Georgia)

1897 edition. "Published for the Proprietress, Mrs. M. E. Atkins, Temple, Texas." (Cited in Tennyson, Plate II, page 27)

1900 edition. "Published for the Proprietress, Mrs. M. E. Atkins, Temple, Texas." This edition has gold-tooling on cover that is identical to the modern editions. It also has a gold-embossed "Primitive Hymns" on the spine. It contains the 1858 Preface and the larger format that is still used today. This edition or possibly the 1897 is the first of the larger format, 15-16 cm in height. It does not contain "The Romish Lady." Even though the last hymn is numbered 705, there are actually 704 hymns in this book. When "The Romish Lady" was dropped, no other hymn was put in for #698, so there is a skip from hymn #697 and #699. (Samford University)

1906 edition. "Published for the Proprietress, Mrs. M. E. Atkins, Temple, Texas." Except for the preface addendum, this edition seems to be identical to the 1900 edition. Mrs. M. E. Atkins addition to the preface reads:

> I wish to add to the above (the 1858 preface) that on the death of my dear mother (Mrs. Benjamin Lloyd) who requested her son (J. C. Lloyd) my former husband, to purchase the type and business from the estate of his father (Elder Benjamin Lloyd) and keep up the publication of the Book, which he did as long as his life was spared, since his death it has been my great and conscientious desire to make the Book without fault as far as possible. I have enlarged the type which makes it now clear and suitable for the aged, as well as the young. I have added five hymns and reinstated the hymn titled "The Romish Lady." My humble prayer to God has been that he would sustain me in all my efforts to keep this Book in its purity. With deepest gratitude to all my friends and patrons I am your humble servant in God. Mrs. M. E. Atkins, Temple, Texas.

Even though the 1906 preface says that "The Romish Lady" was reinstated, it does not appear in this edition of the hymnal. (Library of Congress)

1921 edition. "Published for the proprietors, O. L. Terry, and La V. L. Smith, 1921." This addendum is found at the end of the 1858 Preface:

> Since the death of our dear mother (Mrs. M. E. Atkins), who so earnestly requested that the publication of the Book be kept up and in the family, we wish to say that we have purchased the copyright, stereotype plates, all the claims and everything pertaining to the business from her estate and will continue the publication of the Book under the same style and standard, and it is our sincere desire to give prompt attention to all orders.
>
> Opal Lloyd Terry
> La Verte Lloyd Smith, Manager
> February 4, 1921
> La Mesa, California

After the reinstatement of "The Romish Lady" in this edition, it appears in the first lines index as "The Romish Lady," its title, and not by its first line, "There was a Romish lady, brought up in popery." In this index, the addition of "The Romish Lady" title caused the printer to close up the space between the "S" section and the "T" section.

This version of the hymn book is the one printed in facsimile today by the Primitive Hymns Corporation of Rocky Mount, North Carolina. (Library of Congress)

1923 edition. (Mentioned in a letter from La Verte Smith to O. C. Weaver, 1969)

1926 edition. (Mentioned in a letter from La Verte Smith to O. C. Weaver, 1969)

1929 edition. (Mentioned in a letter from La Verte Smith to O. C. Weaver, 1969)

1930 edition. "Published for the Proprietors, Opal Lloyd Terry and La Verte Lloyd Smith, Granddaughters of Benjamin Lloyd, La Mesa, Calif." (Elon College, North Carolina)

1935 edition. "Published for the Proprietors, Opal Lloyd Terry and La Verte Lloyd Smith, Granddaughters of Benjamin Lloyd, La Mesa, Calif." (Cited in Tennyson, Plate II, page 27)

1939 edition. "Published for the Proprietors, Opal Lloyd Terry and La Verte Lloyd Smith, Granddaughters of Benjamin Lloyd, La Mesa, Calif." (Cited in Tennyson, Plate II, page 27)

1945 edition. (Mentioned in a letter from LaVerte Smith to O. C. Weaver, 1969)

1946 edition. This edition has 700 hymns and was kept in print for Associations such as the Alabaha River Primitive Baptist Association of southern Georgia, who preferred this version of the hymn book . (Information from David Lee)

1952 edition. (Mentioned in a letter from La Verte Smith to O. C. Weaver, 1969)

1954 edition. "Published for the Proprietors, Opal Lloyd Terry and La Verte Lloyd Smith, Granddaughters of Benjamin Lloyd, Box 1135, Beverly Hills, California, 1954." (Don Clark)

1957 edition. (Mentioned in a letter from La Verte Smith to O. C. Weaver, 1969)

1959 edition. "Published for the Proprietors, Opal Lloyd Terry and La Verte Lloyd Smith, Granddaughters of Benj. Lloyd, Box 1105, Whittier, CA." (Bethel Church, Cullman County, Alabama)

1963 edition. "Published for the Proprietors, Opal Lloyd Terry and La Verte Lloyd Smith, Granddaughters of Benj. Lloyd, Box 1105, Whittier, CA." This edition has 700 hymns and was kept in print for associations such as the Alabaha River Primitive Baptist Association of southern Georgia, whose members preferred this version of the hymn book. It has the 1858 and 1921 prefaces. The five hymns that are left out of this hymnal are: #691, "Oh, to be robed and ready"; #690, "The Lord is my Shepherd" (Twenty-third Psalm); #689, "O land of rest for thee I sigh"; #688, "We shall sleep but not forever"; #687, "Rock of Ages." (Information from David Lee)

1966 edition. Published by Opal Lloyd Terry and La Verte Lloyd Smith. (Cited in Tennyson, Plate II, page 27)

1971 edition. This is the first edition published by "The Primitive Hymns Corporation, P. O. Box 92, Rocky Mount, North Carolina 27801." It includes the 1858 preface without the 1921 Terry and Smith preface addition; it is otherwise identical to the 1921 edition. (Don Clark)

1975 edition. This edition was published by the Primitive Hymns Corporation, but has only 700 hymns. It was printed for the Alabaha River Primitive Baptist Association exactly like the 1963 edition of 700 hymns published by Mrs. Smith and Terry. This edition includes the 1858 preface and the 1921 preface addendum. (David Lee)

1978 edition. This edition is identical to the 1971 edition and published by the Primitive Hymns Corporation. (Auburn University)

1986 edition. This edition is identical to the 1971 edition and published by the Primitive Hymns Corporation. (Alabama Public Library Service printout)

1989 edition. This edition is identical to the 1971 edition and published by the Primitive Hymns Corporation. (Joey Brackner)

1996 edition. This edition is identical to the 1971 edition and published by the Primitive Hymns Corporation. (Bethel Church, Cullman County)

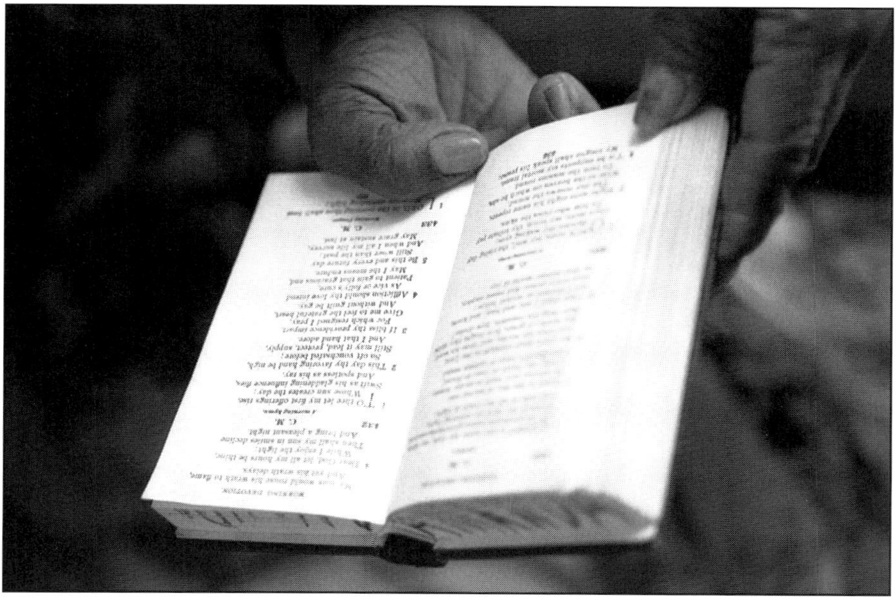

Kim Appel

Around 1900 The Primitive Hymns *was published in the 10x15 cm. format still used today.*

SUGGESTED READINGS AND RECORDINGS

Benson, Louis F. 1962 [1915]. *The English Hymn: Its Development and Use in Worship*. Richmond: John Knox Press.

Chase, Gilbert. 1987. *America's Music: From the Pilgrims to the Present*. Revised 3d ed. New York: McGraw-Hill.

Drummond, Robert Paul. 1989. *A Portion for the Singers*. Atwood, Tennessee: Christian Baptist Library and Publishing Company.

Epstein, Dena. 1977. *Sinful Tunes and Spirituals: Black Folk Music to the Civil War*. Urbana: University of Illinois Press.

Jackson, George Pullen. 1933. *White Spirituals in the Southern Uplands*. Chapel Hill: University of North Carolina Press.

———. 1943. *White and Negro Spirituals: Their Life Span and Kinship*. New York: J.J. Augustin.

Norton, Kay. Forthcoming. *Mercer's "Cluster" of 1810: Baptist Offspring and Southern Midwife*. The College Music Society, Monographs and Bibliographies in American Music Series.

Patterson, Beverly Bush. 1995. *The Sound of the Dove: Singing in Appalachian Primitive Baptist Churches*. Urbana: University of Illinois Press.

———. Forthcoming. Primitive Baptist Singing in the Southern Appalachians. In *American Musical Atlas*, ed. Jeff Todd Titon and Bob Carlin. New York: Schirmer Books.

Peacock, James L., and Ruel W. Tyson, Jr. 1989. *Pilgrims of Paradox: Calvinism and Experience among the Primitive Baptists of the Blue Ridge*. Washington, D. C.: Smithsonian Institution Press.

Pitts, Walter F. 1993. *Old Ship of Zion: The Afro-Baptist Ritual in the African Diaspora*. New York: Oxford University Press.

Sommers, Laurie Kay. Forthcoming. The Okefenokee. In *American Musical Atlas*, ed. Jeff Todd Titon and Bob Carlin. New York: Schirmer Books.

Southern, Eileen. 1983. *Readings in Black American Music*. 2nd ed. New York: W. W. Norton.

———. 1997. *The Music of Black Americans*. Revised 3rd ed. New York: W. W. Norton.

Sutton, Brett, and Peter Hartman, producers. 1982. *Primitive Baptist Hymns of the Blue Ridge*. Sung by congregations in Virginia and North Carolina. Monaural LP recording with booklet. Chapel Hill: University of North Carolina Press.

Temperley, Nicholas. 1981. The Old Way of Singing: Its Origins and Development. *Journal of American Musicological Society* 34:511-44.

Tennyson, Don. 1973. *A Study of Benjamin Lloyd's "The Primitive Hymns."* Master of Church Music Thesis, New Orleans Theological Seminary.

Titon, Jeff Todd, producer. 1997. *Old Regular Baptists: Lined-Out Hymnody from Southeastern Kentucky*. Sung by members of the Indian Bottom Association, Old Regular Baptists, at Defeated Creek Church, Linefork, Kentucky, August 20, 1992, and June 10, 1993. Washington, D.C.: Smithsonian Folkways Recordings, SF CD 40106.

Willett, Henry, ed. 1995. *In the Spirit: Alabama's Sacred Music Traditions*. Montgomery, Alabama: Black Belt Press.

BENJAMIN LLOYD'S HYMN BOOK: A PRIMITIVE BAPTIST SONG TRADITION

NOTES TO THE COMPACT DISC

What happens to the music when congregations sing hymns without musical instruments from a word-only hymn book for a century or more? This compact disc provides an aural answer to that question.

Here we have singing by Primitive Baptists who sing from Lloyd's *Primitive Hymns* in Alabama, Georgia, North Carolina, and West Virginia. The geographical range of this recording does not begin to cover the 30 states in which people sing from Lloyd, yet in this small sample we hear such a diversity of styles that we can only begin to imagine the myriad approaches to the hymns by Primitive Baptists across the nation.

Many of the tunes presented here are of unknown origin and were sung with secular as well as sacred texts in the British Isles prior to the colonization of America. When the compilers of hymn books began to include musical notation, they wrote down tunes that had been orally transmitted prior to that. In churches that continued to use word-only hymn books, however, the tunes were still subject to variations brought about by the folk process. Thus on this compact disc you will hear tunes that have changed to a degree that they bear no resemblance to any written in hymn books, some that faintly suggest a written tune, and some that are the same as those in tunebooks.

The diversity of styles includes singing by both black and white Primitive Baptist congregations. The African American performances on this compact disc are largely unaffected by books with musical notation while most of those by white singers are influenced in varying degrees by such tunebooks as B. F. White's *The Sacred Harp* (orig.1844), William Walker's *Christian Harmony* (1866), Elder C. H. Cayce's *The Good Old Songs* (1913), and the *Old School Hymnal* (ca. 1930, published by various Primitive Baptist elders, most recently J. A. Monsees). The first two are shape-note books, written in three and four-part harmony, and meant for musical instruction and social singing outside of the worship service. Many southern Primitive Baptists are shape-note singers and host annual singings at their churches. *The Good Old Songs* and the *Old School Hymnal* are hymnbooks used in services at many Primitive Baptist churches as well as at gatherings of singers. All four contain many of the same hymns that are in Lloyd's hymnbook and affect the choice of tunes used with particular texts, the harmonies sung and choruses added. However, those who sing from Lloyd's *Primitive Hymns* believe that the word-only book allows the spirit to choose the best tune for the moment and do not allow themselves to be dominated by musical notation in hymn books used by fellow Primitive Baptists.

Another influence on the singing is the practice of forming associations. Each Primitive Baptist church governs itself and is not under the supervision of a denominational hierarchy, yet many choose to formally associate with other Primitive Baptist congregations in the vicinity. As most congregations meet once a month, their members may visit other churches in the association on other Sundays and attend three-day annual meetings with them. These meetings are also attended by representatives of "corresponding" associations, some from other states and some which use hymn books other than Lloyd's. The interaction between congregations and associations leads to musical cross-pollination. Singers discover new ways to sing hymns and different tune-text combinations. Though by definition Primitive Baptists are a conservative group they do allow changes to occur in the way they sing.

This compact disc includes singing from Lloyd's hymnal in church, at home, and at social gatherings. One selection features a concert performance by a non-Primitive Baptist demonstrating an Appalachian style of hymn singing done in her grandparents' church. Each track is identified by the hymn number given in the 705-hymn version of Lloyd's hymnal, the edition currently published by the Primitive Hymns Corporation. The hymn number is followed by the first line of the text which, in keeping with nineteenth century practice, serves as its title. Following the first line is an abbreviation signifying the hymn's meter. Meter abbreviations indicate the number of syllables per line of text in one stanza of a hymn. They are used to match hymns to suitable tunes. A hymn written in common meter (C.M.) alternates between 8 and 6 syllables per line and fits any common meter tune. Long meter (L.M.) has 8 syllables per line and short meter (S.M.) has 6,6,8, and 6 syllables per line. A text in the particular meter (P.M) has its own tune. The verses sung in each performance are reproduced in these notes directly from Lloyd's *Primitive Hymns*.

The Lee Family

1. #595, "Ye objects of sense, and enjoyments of time" (11,8)

2. #45, "Saw ye my Savior" (P.M.)

3. #152, "I walked abroad one morning fair" (L.M.)

4. #206, "The Christians of old, united in one" (P.M. 10s)

Sung by Lee family members and friends at the home of David and Kathy Lee on November 22, 1997, Hoboken, Georgia. Singers include David and Kathy Lee, Clarke and Julie Lee, Tollie and Ramona Lee, Johnny and Delorese Lee, Brian Lee, Rachel and Bryant Lee and Alvin Johnson. Recorded by Joyce Cauthen and Joey Brackner.

The Lee family members on this recording are part of a large family with a legendary singing tradition. Their ancestors settled on Cowhouse Island of the Okefenokee Swamp in southeast Georgia at the beginning of the nineteenth century. There they farmed, dipped turpentine, sawed timber, cut crossties and worshipped as Primitive Baptists. They sang from Lloyd's *Primitive Hymns* and *The Sacred Harp*. David Lee remembers gatherings where Lee family singers numbered in the hundreds. When the children got too loud or were fussing, David's grandfather would call them in to sing hymns; the adults would join in and they would sing for hours. If they were called to the table to sing, they knew they were going to sing from *The Sacred Harp*, or the "note book" as they called it. More often they sang from memory or out of the "word book," their term for Lloyd's hymn book. Clarke Lee explained the relationship between the two. When singing from *Primitive Hymns*, they frequently use tunes and harmonies written in *The Sacred Harp*. However, their timing is more flexible and the harmonies they sing may or may not be the same as those in the note book, depending on what the next person is singing, the key in which it is being sung and how well one remembers the written version.

The Lees do not wed texts to tunes. Most hymns, other than those in the particular meter, may be sung to any tune of the same meter. In the course of a year a hymn may have a different tune each time it is sung, depending on who starts it and the context. About ten of the tunes they sing are not in *The Sacred Harp*. So that those will not be forgotten, Philip Reeves and Clarke and David Lee have transcribed them in shape-note musical notation and self-published them as *The Pilgrim's Harp*, better known as "the brown book."

David Lee and most of those gathered for this singing grew up in the High Bluff Primitive Baptist Church. Like other churches in this very conservative Crawfordite sub-sect of the denomination, High Bluff has seen very little physical change since it was built in 1821. It has no electricity, heat, insulation, or indoor plumbing and its leadership refuses to acknowledge daylight savings time in holding church services. After Lloyd's *Primitive Hymns* was expanded from 700 to 705 hymns in 1906, the congregation refused to accept these changes and since that time have had special printings made using plates from a pre-1906 edition. They have maintained a distinctive slow style of singing with a bagpipe-like drone and continue the centuries-old practice of lining out hymns during the worship service.

However, with the passage of time the large family gatherings ceased, and with them the singings. David and Clarke Lee had grown up singing from Lloyd's *Primitive Hymns* and *The Sacred Harp* in the 1950s and 1960s, when other children were watching TV and listening to rock and roll on the radio. "This is all we did," said David Lee. "We sang these songs. We didn't sing no other songs, we didn't sing out of no other book, we didn't listen to no other music." With singing being such a strong part of their identity, they could not bear its absence.

Much to the delight of the national community of *Sacred Harp* singers, a small number of Lees in the mid-1990s began to attend singings outside of the family. They enjoyed the fellowship, though at first the music seemed alien to them, being accented differently and sung at a much faster pace. Since that time they have reestablished the annual Hoboken *Sacred Harp* Convention and have attended singings across the nation at the invitation of singers eager to learn the Hoboken style. Wherever they go they have encouraged sessions devoted to singing from Lloyd's *Primitive Hymns* and have contributed to a revival of interest in the hymn book.

Though this branch of the Lee family is generous with its music, they do not allow church services to be recorded and feel that it is inappropriate to line out hymns at social gatherings. Thus we do not have examples of their style of singing in church on this compact disc. The hymns reproduced here were sung after a bountiful supper shared by family and friends at the home of David and Kathy Lee. They are seriously devout and revere Lloyd's *Primitive Hymns* as being "sacred right behind the Bible," but they have fun at such singing sessions. There is much hearty laughter, teasing, and retelling of family stories while they turn pages and ready themselves to launch with whole heart and full voice into the next hymn.

"Ye Objects of Sense" was written by Benjamin Francis in 1795. This hymn appears in Cayce's *Good Old Songs*, paired with the tune "Song of Texas," to which the Lee's tune bears some resemblance.

1 YE objects of sense, and enjoyments of time,
Which oft have delighted my heart;
I soon shall exchange you for views more sublime,
For joys that shall never depart.

2 Thou Lord of the day, and thou queen of the night,
To me ye no longer are known;
I soon shall behold, with increasing delight,
A sun that shall never go down.

"Saw ye my Savior" is set to "a Scotch air" in *The Olive Leaf,* a shape-note book complied in Georgia in 1878. The tune is the same as that sung by the Lee family. George Pullen Jackson suggests that this tune was used with Scottish and English ballads such as "Saw ye my Father?" and "The Grey Cock."

1 SAW ye my Saviour, saw ye my Saviour
Saw ye my Saviour and God?
Oh! he died on Calvary,
To atone for you and me,
And to purchase our pardon with blood.

2 He was extended, he was extended,
Shamefully nailed to the cross;
Oh! he bowed his head and died;
Thus my Lord was crucified,
To atone for a world that was lost.

8 'I will forgive them, I will forgive them
Says the kind Father to thee;
'Let them now return to thee,
And be reconciled to me,
And eternally saved they shall be.'

"I walked abroad one morning fair" is included in "the brown book" as a tune which the Lees believe is not printed in tune-books.

1 I WALKED abroad one morning fair,
When odors sweetly balmed the air;
And birds their artless notes did sing,
To welcome in the cheerful spring.
2 Surveying nature all around,
The scene with wonder did abound;
But while my ravished eyes were charmed,
An inward voice my soul alarmed:
3 'Could you all nature comprehend,
You'd better learn to know your end;
These beauties which you now survey
Will, like yourself, soon pass away.

The Lees sang the first verse of "The Christians of old, united in one" in the slow meditative way it has always been sung in their family. After some conversation they sang a gospel version of it they learned in visits to Alabama. That version appears later on Track #7 as sung by Smyrna Primitive Baptist Church and the text is given at that point in the notes.

For more information on the Lee family's style of singing, see Laurie Kay Sommers, "The Okefenokee" in *American Musical Atlas*, Jeff Todd Titon, ed., MacMillan, forthcoming. George Pullen Jackson's comments on "Saw ye my Savior" are in *Spiritual Folk-Songs of Early America* (New York: J. J. Augustin, 1937), 44-45.

New Jerusalem Primitive Baptist Church

5. #440, "The day is past and gone" (S.M.)

Sung by the congregation of New Jerusalem Primitive Baptist Church, Bessemer, Alabama, April 21, 1996. Lined out by Elder Frank Eatman, Jr.

New Jerusalem Primitive Baptist Church is tucked into a residential neighborhood of Bessemer, Alabama. Though its members reside in the cities of Bessemer and Birmingham, it retains strong ties with rural Primitive Baptist churches of West Alabama through its affiliation with the Sipsey River Association. This selection was recorded in a regular Sunday morning service with an attendance of about forty. It is a "Dr. Watts" style hymn, sung slowly and lined out.

Prior to his sermon, Elder Frank Eatman, Jr., requested that the congregation join him in singing "The day is past and gone." They slowly sang those words, giving four beats to each syllable, then continued through two verses, which Elder Eatman called out two lines at a time.

The tune used with this text by John Leland is one that the churches of the Sipsey River Association sing with all short meter hymns, such as "Beside the gospel pool" and "Blessed be the tie that binds." A transcription of it appears in William Dargan's essay in this publication. Dargan and others have suggested that it may have roots in the tune "Idumea" which can be heard on Track #10, "Hungry, and faint, and poor," as sung at Little Hope Primitive Baptist Church.

1 THE day is past and gone,
The evening shades appear;
O may we all remember well
The night of death is near.

2 We lay our garments by,
Upon our beds to rest,
So death will soon disrobe us all
Of what we here possess.

See William Dargan's transcription of this performance of #440, "The day is past and gone," on page 40 of this volume. See essays by Joyce Cauthen and William Dargan in this publication for more on "Dr. Watts" singing and the Sipsey River Association.

Smyrna Primitive Baptist Church

6. #390, "I would, but cannot sing" (S.M.)

7. #206, "The Christians old, united in one" (P.M. 10s)

Sung by the congregation of Smyrna Primitive Baptist Church, Goodwater, Alabama, March 14, 1998.

Smyrna, Mt. Zion, and Bethlehem Primitive Baptist Churches belong to the Hillabee Association. Prior to 1870, the Hillabee churches were part of the Beulah Association, of which Benjamin Lloyd was a founding member.

Members of the three congregations along with others from the Lower Wetumpka Association regularly worship at each other's churches, and all come early for a half-hour or more of singing before the worship service begins. There are many good song leaders among the deacons and elders who take their places in the pews to the side of the pulpit. The singers call out the numbers of the hymns they would like to sing and the leader honors each request. If he does not know a particular hymn, he passes leadership to one who does. Many of them grew up singing from *The Sacred Harp* also, and Smyrna hosts *Sacred Harp* singings on the third Sundays in April and September.

Elder Bufrey Dean, pastor of Oak Grove Primitive Baptist Church in Sylacauga, led both hymns included on the compact disc. "I would, but cannot sing," written by John Newton, is set to a tune identified as "Sing to Me of Heaven" in *The Sacred Harp*.

1 I WOULD, but cannot sing;
I would, but cannot pray;
For Satan meets me when I try,
And frights my soul away.

2 I would, but can't repent,
Though I endeavor oft;
This stony heart can ne'er relent,
Till Jesus makes it soft.

3 I would, but cannot love,
Though wooed by love divine;
No arguments have power to move
A soul so base as mine.

4 I would, but cannot rest
In God's most holy will;
I know what he appoints is best,
Yet murmur at it still.

PAUSE.

5 O could I but believe,
Then all would easy be;
I would, but cannot:—Lord, relieve,
My help must come from thee.

6 But if indeed I would,
Though I can nothing do,
Yet the desire is something good,
For which my praise is due.

7 By nature prone to ill,
Till thine appointed hour,
I was as destitute of will,
As now I am of power.

8 Wilt thou not crown at length
The work thou hast begun,
And with a will afford me strength
In all thy ways to run?

"The Christians of old, united in one," which Lloyd described as "a review of primitive days," is a favorite of Lloyd hymn singers because its describes the simple, modest, solid and worshipful kind of lifestyle they strive to achieve. On Track #4, the Lees sing it in the old way, with roots in the psalm-singing of the New England colonies. Here the Smyrna congregtion sings it in call-and-response form. Churches of the Hillabee Association have sung it in this style for as long as anyone can remember, while others, like the Lee family and singers in north Alabama have recently begun singing it this way.

1 THE Christians of old, united in one,
As sheep in a fold were never alone,
As birds of a feather they flocked to their nest,
And sheltered together in Jesus's breast:

2 However employed. their joy was the same,
They never were cloyed in hymning the Lamb;
Their sole recreation to sing of his praise,
And publish salvation by Jesus's grace.

3 Small learning they had, and wanted no more,
Not many could read, but all could adore;
No help from the college or school they received,
Content with his knowledge in whom they believed.

4 No riches had they but riches of grace,
No fondness for play or passion for praise,
No moments of leisure for trifling employs,
Possessed of the treasure in God to rejoice.

5 Men, in their own eyes were children again,
And children were wise and solid as men;
The women were fearful of nothing but sin,
Their hearts were all cheerful, their consciences clean.

6 Wrapt up in the Lord, his service and love,
They lived and adored like angels above;
And blest with his presence, their lives they laid down,
And now with their Saviour inherit the crown.

Shiloh Primitive Baptist Church

8. #695, "Dark and thorny is the desert" (8s and 7s)

Recorded at the Shiloh Primitive Baptist Association Annual Meeting on the third weekend of October, 1997, Elkin, North Carolina, by Drew Armstrong.

9. #270, "O may I worthy prove to see" (L.M.)

Recorded at the Shiloh Primitive Baptist Association Annual Meeting on the third weekend of October, 1998, Elkin, North Carolina, by Drew Armstrong.

Shiloh is a small, young Primitive Baptist Association consisting of two congregations, Shiloh in Elkin, North Carolina, and True Faith in Winson-Salem. Combined membership for both congregations is fifteen, though twenty-five or more attend regular services. It was founded in 1979 by Elder Ronnie Houser, who grew up in Sandy Ridge, the state's oldest and largest African American Primitive Baptist association. Elder Houser was only thirty-one at the time he founded Shiloh in a renovated store building, yet he set it up as a conservative church which does not sanction choirs and musical instruments in worship services, Sunday school classes, usher boards and other church activities which are not specifically mentioned in the Bible. However, women are allowed to participate more fully in church administration and song-leading than in other conservative Primitive Baptist churches. These recordings were made at the annual association meeting attended by about 150 people from the two Shiloh churches plus corresponding associations in Virginia, Kentucky, and North Carolina.

The Shiloh congregation sings solely from Lloyd's *Primitive Hymns* in the style generations of Housers have sung. Elder Houser's mother, Mother Margaret Houser, was a strong hymn raiser. His sister, Mother Gail Whittington, can be heard leading hymn #270 on this compact disc. Though they do not sing in the slow, embellished "Dr. Watt's" style, they do line out hymns. This is done out of custom rather than necessity, as the singers have hymnals and call out the lines along with the leader before singing them.

"Dark and thorny is the desert" is mentioned in a biography of Harriet Tubman written in 1869 by Sarah H. Bradford. Bradford describes an incident where Tubman sings the hymn to identify herself to hiding slaves. Hers is a folk version of the hymn in which three verses are mixed with two verses from another hymn. Apparently Tubman sang it in "Dr. Watts" style, for Bradford wrote, "The air sung to these words was so wild, so full of plaintive minor strains and unexpected quavers, that I would defy any white person to learn it, and often as I heard it, it was to me a constant surprise."

1 DARK and thorny is the desert
Through which pilgrims make their [way
But beyond this vale of sorrows
Lie the fields of endless day;
Fiends, loud howling through the desert,
Make them tremble as they go;
And the fiery darts of Satan
Often bring their courage low.

2 O young soldiers, are you weary
Of the troubles of the way?
Does your strength begin to fail you,
And your vigor to decay?
Jesus, Jesus will go with you;
He will lead you to his throne;
He who dyed his garments for you
And the wine-press trod alone.

3 He whose thunder shakes creation;
He who bids the planets roll;
He who rides upon the tempest,
And whose sceptre sways the whole;
Round him are ten thousand angels,
Ready to obey command;
They are always hovering round you,
Till you reach the heavenly land.

4 There, on flowery hills of pleasure,
In the fields of endless rest,
Love, and joy, and peace, shall ever
Reign in triumph in your breast.
Who can paint those scenes of glory,
Where the ransomed dwell on high?
Where the golden harps for ever
Sound redemption through the sky?

Elder Houser led "O may I worthy prove to see," giving out one line at a time, a common practice in the association. He does not sing the chorus which is indicated in the hymn book—"And I'll sing glory, glory, And glory be to God on high," but sings all nine verses, four of which are included here.

1 O MAY I worthy prove to see
The saints in full prosperity;
To see the bride, the glittering bride,
Close seated by the Saviour's side.

CHORUS—And I'll sing glory, glory,
And glory be to God on high.

2 O may I find some humble seat
Beneath my dear Redeemer's feet!
A servant, as before he's been,
I'll sing salvation to my King.

3 I'm glad that I am born to die ;
From grief and woe my soul shall fly ;
Bright angels shall convey me home,
Away to the new Jerusalem.

4 I'll praise him while he gives me breath;
I hope to praise him after death ;
I hope to praise him when I die,
And shout salvation as I fly.

See William Dargan's transcription of #695, "Dark and thorny is the desert," on page 44 of this volume. Sarah H. Bradford's *Harriet, the Moses of her People*, was first published as *Scenes in the Life of Harriet Tubman* in 1869.

Little Hope Primitive Baptist Church

10. #492, "Hungry, and faint, and poor" (S.M.)

11. #662, "Sweet to rejoice in lively hope" (C.M.)

Sung by Ola Deason Meadows, Don Smith, Toney Smith, Carver Deason, Mary Deason, Art and Ann Deason, Clara Deason Smith, LaTisha Smith Crocker, Doug Wyers, Dona Smith Kornegay, Deborah Feaster, Luke Smith, Kristi McKenzie, Keith Meggs Crocker, W. T. Wyers, Mildred Wyers, Elvin Deason Morris, Earnestine Deason Thompson, Arthur and Dottie Parrish, Gail Morris Fuller at Little Hope Primitive Baptist Church, Eoline (Bibb County), Alabama, November 19, 1995. Recorded by Joyce Cauthen.

After their Sunday service at Little Hope Primitive Baptist, Deason family members and friends spread food out on tables in the church yard for a quick meal before returning to the church to sing for this recording. The Deason family is filled with good singers and is well known for its involvement with *Christian Harmony*, a seven shape note book originally published in 1866. They have revised it, composed new songs for it, kept it in print and taught singing schools based on it. Singing from *Christian Harmony* is central to their large annual family reunions. They also have a strong connection with "the hymn book" or "Lloyd's hymn book," as they call it. Elder Donald Smith, whose mother is a Deason, said, "We received the use of the *Primitive Hymns* from our forefathers at Little Hope and have never (so far as I can find record) considered changing or dropping the use of it." The fact that the word-only book does not dictate tunes provides more opportunity for the spirit to enter the singing. Says Smith, "We always refer to 'raising a hymn' in the hymn book and sometimes we have felt the spirit as much in the tune selected or raised as we have in the singing of the hymn itself. This is hard to explain, but I will say this—some of the hymns at times are special because at the moment the tune fits the sentiments of the poetry in it."

Hymn #492, "Hungry, and faint, and poor," is often used to open the preaching service. Elder Smith feels that the solemn minor tune "Idumea" fits the sentiments of John Newton's text well. "Idumea" was first printed in Ananias Davisson's *Kentucky Harmony* (1815) and subsequently appeared in most southern tunebooks. According to George Pullen Jackson, it also was used with secular ballads, such as "Lord Lovel," and some believe it may be the basis for the tune heard on Track #5, as sung in African American congregations.

1 HUNGRY, and faint, and poor
Behold us, Lord, again
Assembled at thy mercy's door,
Thy bounty to obtain.

2 Thy word invites us nigh,
Or we must starve indeed ;
For we no money have to buy,
No righteousness to plead.

3 The food our spirits want,
Thy hand alone can give ;
O hear the prayer of faith and grant
That we may eat and live.

Although #662, "Sweet to rejoice in lively hope," has no chorus printed in Lloyd's hymn book, the singers here added one associated with that hymn in *The Old School Hymnal* and *The Good Old Songs*. As written in both tunebooks, they sing "rising day" in the chorus rather than "judgement day," because of their belief in predestination.

1 SWEET to rejoice in lively hope,
That, when my change shall come
Angels will hover round my bed
And waft my spirit home.

2 There shall my disembodied soul
View Jesus and adore;
Be with his likeness satisfied,
And grieve and sin no more.

3 Shall see him wear that very flesh
On which my guilt was lain;
His love intense, his merit fresh,
As though but newly slain.

4 Soon, too, my slumbering dust shall hear
The trumpet's quickening sound,
And by my Saviour's power rebuilt,
At his right hand be found.

5 If such the views which grace unfold,
Weak as it is below,
What rapture must the church above
In Jesus' presence know!

6 O may the unction of these truths
For ever with me stay;
Till from her sinful rage dismissed
My spirit flies away.

Anne Kimzey

Keith Crocker, Douglas Wyers, Clara Deason Smith, Elder Donald Smith, Latisha Smith Crocker and Kevin Crocker gather at Little Hope Primitive Baptist Church in Eoline, Alabama, to sing from Lloyd's hymn book and Christian Harmony *during the Deason family reunion.*

See also Anne H. F. Kimzey, "The Deasons: a Christian Harmony Family," in *In the Spirit: Alabama's Sacred Music Traditions*, ed. Henry Willett, (Montgomery, Alabama: Black Belt Press, 1995), 56-61, and Joey Brackner's article in this publication. George Pullen Jackson's comments on "Idumea" are in *Spiritual Folk-Songs of Early America* (New York: J. J. Augustin, 1937), 155-56.

Jesse Allison, Doc Reed, and Vera Hall

12. #3, "Amazing grace, how sweet the sound" (C.M.)

Sung by Jesse Allison, Doc Reed, and Vera Hall, May, 1939, Livingston, Alabama, recorded by John A. and Ruby T. Lomax. Digital master and noise reduction by Steve Grauberger at the Alabama Center for Traditional Culture.

This selection was one of many songs recorded in the Livingston, Alabama, area by John A. and Ruby T. Lomax, with the assistance of Livingston native Ruby Pickens Tartt. In 1939 Mrs. Lomax described their work in a press release for the local newspaper:

> Two years ago, while Mr. Lomax was supervising the gathering of folk materials for the Federal Writers Project, Mr. Lomax and his wife worked in Livingston, Alabama, with Negro "Songsters" who were introduced to them by Mrs. Ruby

Pickens Tartt. On that visit more than a hundred songs were recorded. The names of some of these singers are well-known in the Music Division of the Library of Congress, particularly Doc Reed and Vera Hall, whose records of spirituals are the pride of the Folk Song Archive. (From files in the American Folklife Center of the Library of Congress)

On their return visit in 1939 the Lomaxes brought better recording equipment and, guided by Mrs. Tartt, they filled twenty twelve-inch records with spirituals, play party songs, work songs, lullabies, and hymns. Among them was this recording of "Amazing Grace."

Mrs. Lomax wrote that Doc Reed and Vera Hall "are good singers of the old style spirituals, are perfect in 'seconding'—'following after,' they call it—and they know many songs." As followers rather than leaders of hymns sung in the "Dr. Watts" style, they may have suggested Jesse Allison as a good hymn raiser for a recording. A deacon at Mt. Pilgrim Primitive Baptist Church, Allison was well-known for his clear lining out and the spirituality of his singing.

George Pullen Jackson listened to this recording of "Amazing Grace" prior to the publication of *White and Negro Spirituals* in 1943 and identified the tune as "Pisgah." However, this writer recognizes it as "New Britain," the tune most often associated with John Newton's beloved hymn. It is sung more quickly than most "Dr. Watts" hymns at Mt. Pilgrim, as exemplified on the following track. This is not an indication that the congregation is singing more slowly today than it did in 1939. According to Sister Bertha Bell, a life-long member of Mt. Pilgrim, they have always sung slowly, and may have sung even slower in the past. "Amazing Grace" is customarily sung in a more upbeat fashion.

1 AMAZING grace! how sweet the sound
That saved a wretch like me!
I once was lost, but now am found,
Was blind, but now I see.

2 'Twas grace that taught my heart to fear,
And grace my fears relieved:
How precious did that grace appear,
The hour I first believed!

See William Dargan's transcription of this performance of #3, "Amazing Grace how sweet the sound," on page 41 of this volume. George Pullen Jackson's comments on "Amazing Grace" are in *White and Negro Spirituals: Their Life Span and Kinship* (New York: J. J. Augustin, 1943), 249-51.

Mt. Pilgrim Primitive Baptist Church

13. #241, "That doleful night before his death" (C.M.)

Sung by the congregation of Mt. Pilgrim Primitive Baptist Church, Livingston, Alabama, September 13, 1998. Recorded by Joyce Cauthen.

Mt. Pilgrim Primitive Baptist Church is a small wooden structure built in 1922 next to the one-room Rosenwald school that served the African American children of the community at that time. Once part of the Sipsey River Association, in 1951 Mt. Pilgrim joined the Goodwill Association, a group of more progressive churches which have choirs, musical instruments, Sunday school classes, usher boards, revivals, and other church-related activities not encouraged in the older association. In recent years it has not been affiliated with any association.

Mt. Pilgrim's choir is made up of adults, teenagers, and young children. They sing spirituals and gospel songs as featured numbers and during collections. Most of their singing is *a cappella* due to a lack of instrumentalists in the congregation, but they have no objections to pianos, guitars or drums when available. Though this music adds a modern element not found in the churches of the Sipsey River Association, the congregation still sings a number of hymns in the old way with the encouragement of Elder Lieutenant Whitfield. According to Deacon Edward Bell, Elder Whitfield is a particularly good hymn raiser. Almost anyone can "give out" or "verse out" a hymn, says Bell, but to "raise" a hymn involves knowing the tune and setting a pitch that the congregation can sing well.

Elder Whitfield is a champion of the "Dr. Watts" style of singing, which he feels is best at stirring the heart and mind of the individual. He heard his grandfather and mother sing hymns in the old way, and when he was converted at the age of seventeen, he prayerfully dedicated himself to mastering the art of hymn singing. He listened closely to Jesse Allison, Josh and Rob Boyd and other well-known hymn singers of the area and learned the tunes to which common, long and short meter hymns are sung. Feeling it would be a tragedy if the "Dr. Watts" tradition were not carried on, he uses every opportunity to sing hymns with the young people of his church.

Here Elder Whitfield leads #241, "That doleful night before his death," written by Joseph Hart, to set an appropriate tone for the communion and footwashing service that follows.

1 THAT doleful night before his death,
The Lamb for sinners slain
Did, almost with his latest breath
This solemn feast ordain.

See William Dargan's transcription of this performance of #241, "That doleful night before his death," on page 45 of this volume.

Ginny Hawker

14. #333, "From every stormy wind that blows" (C.M.)

Sung by Ginny Hawker, August 5, 1997, Augusta Heritage Center of Davis and Elkins College, Elkins, West Virginia. Recorded by Bill Dudley; clone transfer by Flawn Williams. Used courtesy of Augusta Heritage Center.

Ginny Hawker is a performer and presenter of traditional music. A strong harmony singer, she has made recordings with Kay Justice, Hazel Dickens, Carol Elizabeth Jones, and husband Tracy Schwarz. She is director of the West Virginia Folk Festival at Glenville and also director of Vocal Week at the Augusta Heritage Center.

Ms. Hawker's grandparents were members of Old Mill Primitive Baptist Church in Pittsylvania County outside of Danville, Virginia. They lived next to the church and looked after the building. As a child Hawker attended church with them and remembers the congregation moving among each other shaking hands as they sang, often with tears flowing.

When her immediate family moved to the Eastern Shore of Virginia they no longer attended Primitive Baptist services and Hawker lost contact with their way of singing until she was an adult. Remembering the special sound and wanting to be able to sing it, she sought out those who could teach her, in particular Mable Martin of Chilhowie, Virginia. From her visits with Primitive Baptist singers she learned that

> keying is crucial because you are singing in unison. Sometimes the women would sing an octave higher so you would get ringing high notes from the women. As the melody would go up, the women might hold on to the high note they liked. The men would do that when it went down. So you'd have a little harmony or some tension for a beat or two—a hovering of a note. They sang slowly and took a lot of breath, wherever they needed it. They put a little jump or seraph on the ends of notes. [West Virginia fiddler] Melvin Wine calls it 'the little yip.'

Hawker sings from a well worn, rebound copy of Lloyd's *Primitive Hymns* given to her by Annie Maude Hawker, her aunt. "You can always tell which were her favorite hymns," said Hawker, "because she dipped snuff and had tobacco stains on her fingers. There are tobacco stains at the bottom of those pages."

On a visit to her grandparents' church after long years away Hawker was disappointed to find the congregation now using music books. Their singing lacked the vocal embellishments she remembered and did not seem as heartfelt. Fearing that some of the older styles of Primitive Baptist singing are disappearing, Hawker now sings them in performances when appropriate. She sang this version of "Mercy Seat" in a concert for students of traditional music and crafts at an Augusta Heritage Center workshop. Shortly before the performance, she was told that a friend of hers in the audience had been diagnosed with a terminal disease. She dedicated this hymn to her and changed some of the words as she sang to make them more comforting than Hugh Stowell's text.

1 FROM every stormy wind that blows,
From every swelling tide of woes,
There is a calm, a sure retreat—
'Tis found beneath the mercy-seat.
2 There is a place where Jesus sheds
The oil of gladness on our heads;
A place of all on earth most sweet—
It is the blood-bought mercy-seat.
3 There is a scene where spirits blend,
Where friend holds fellowship with friend;
Though sundered far, by faith they meet
Around one common mercy-seat.

5 There, there on eagles' wings we soar,
And sin and sense seem all no more;
And heaven comes down our souls to greet
And glory crowns the mercy-seat.
6 O let my hand forget her skill,
My tongue be silent, cold, and still;
This bounding heart forget to beat,
If I forget the mercy-seat.

Amanda Smith and Ella Pearl White

15. #263, "What wondrous love is this" (P.M.)

Sung by Amanda Smith and Ella Pearl White at the home of Amanda Smith, Loachapoka, Alabama, January 30, 1998, recorded by Joyce Cauthen.

Amanda Smith and Ella Pearl White are considered authorities on hymn singing by fellow members of Mt. Hebrew Primitive Baptist Church and the Spring Hill Union Association in east Alabama. The two sisters have a long family history in the church and know its music intimately. Their great grandmother and her son attended white Primitive Baptist churches before African Americans formed separate churches in the area. Grandfathers on both sides of the family were Primitive Baptist elders and their grandmother, mother and aunts were all active in the church. Most of Amanda Smith's children are members of Mt. Hebrew and one son is a deacon there.

Smith sometimes sits and reads hymns as if they are poems, and she sings them as she goes about her daily life. "I was outside burning bushes yesterday and singing. My little great granddaughter is three and she knows these songs from other songs. The minute I start singing one she wants to shake hands." Smith was referring to the practice of "fellowshipping" while hymns are sung in church. "We do it with one or two hands depending on the spirit.

If we know the song and don't need the books, we lay them down and shake with both hands."

In the Spring Hill Union Association, common, short and long meter hymns may be sung in the slow, lined out "Dr. Watts" style. When Amanda Smith and Ella Pearl White sing in this style they call out the lines together before singing them. When they sing from other meters, however, they seldom line them out. For these they may use tunes similar to those sung in the white churches that their ancestors once attended. Here they sing "Wondrous Love" to the tune that has long been associated with that text in shape-note books, but with melodic and rhythmic variations that have occurred over more than a century of oral transmission.

1 WHAT wondrous love is this,
O my soul ! O my soul !
What wondrous love is this,
O my soul !
What wondrous love is this,
That caused the Lord of bliss
To bear the dreadful curse,
For my soul, for my soul,
To bear the dreadful curse,
For my soul !

2 When I was sinking down,
Sinking down, sinking down,
When I was sinking down,
Sinking down,
When I was sinking down,
Beneath God's righteous frown
Christ laid aside his crown
For my soul, for my soul,
Christ laid aside his crown
For my soul.

3 Ye winged seraphs, fly,
Bear the news, bear the news,
Ye winged seraphs fly,
Bear the news;
Ye winged seraphs, fly,
Like comets through the sky,
Fill vast eternity
with the news, with the news
Fill vast eternity
With the news.

4 To God and to the Lamb,
I will sing, I will sing,
To God and to the Lamb,
I will sing :
To God and to the Lamb,
And to the great I AM,
While millions Join the theme,
I will sing, I will sing,
While millions join the theme,
I will sing.

See William Dargan's transcription of this performance of #263, "What wondrous love is this," on page 39 of this volume.

Mt. Hebrew Primitive Baptist Church

16. #382, "While sorrows encompass me round" (8s and 11s)

Sung by the congregation of Mt. Hebrew Primitive Baptist Church, Notasulga, Alabama, July 20, 1997. Recorded and digitally mastered by Steve Grauberger at the Alabama Center for Traditional Culture.

Mt. Hebrew Primitive Baptist Church belongs to the Spring Hill Union Association founded in 1892. Its five churches are in the vicinity of Tuskegee and Auburn, Alabama. Elder Thomas Peterson of that association says that they sing from Lloyd's hymn book because it is more spiritual than others. As occurs with all who sing from it, there are times that no one can get the tune or pitch of a hymn right. When this happens, according to Peterson, they will say, "The spirit of the Lord is not there. We'll leave this alone because we're not being inspired by the spirit of the Lord to sing it." At other times "you feel like the Lord is tuning you to sing. Sometimes you can feel the Holy Spirit in the whole house and it's uplifting, everybody blending together." He feels that musical instruments and written music take something away from the spirit.

Spring Hill Union Association does not allow women to lead hymns, even though some of its strongest singers are women. However, in recent years it has become customary for everyone to line out hymns together since this practice is no longer a necessity, but an honored tradition. Only common, long, and short meter hymns are lined out. These may be sung in "Dr. Watts" style, though at a quicker pace than others heard on this compact disc, or "in concert," meaning they are sung straight through without stop. Hymns written in particular meter, 8s and 11s and other meters are usually sung in concert. The singers of the Spring Hill Union have a good stock of tunes in various meters, such as the one heard here with "While sorrows encompass me round," written by Caleb Taylor. They use this tune with all other texts written in the 8s and 11s meter. The tune "Idumea," which has an identical melodic contour but different meter, was used for this text in #339 of *The Old School Hymnal*.

1 WHILE sorrows encompass me round,
And endless distresses I see,
Astonished, I cry, can a mortal be found
Surrounded with troubles like me?

2 Few minutes in praise I enjoy,
And they are succeeded by pain;
If a moment in praising of God I employ,
I have hours again to complain.

3 Oh! when shall my sorrows subside?
Oh! when shall my sufferings cease?
Oh! when to the bosom of Christ be conveyed
To the regions of glory and peace?

4 O may I, prepared for that day,
When Christ shall descend from above,
Be filled with his presence, go shouting away
To the arms of my heavenly love.
5 The spirit to glory conveyed,
My body laid low in the ground,
I wish not a tear on my grave to be shed,
But all join in praising around.
6 No sorrow be vented that day,
When Jesus has called me home,
But,singing and shouting,let each brother say
'He's gone from the evil to come.'

See William Dargan's transcription of this performance of #382, "While sorrows encompass me round," on page 44 of this volume.

Oak Grove Primitive Baptist Church

17. #200, "Come, we that love the Lord" (S.M.)

Sung at the annual meeting of Oak Grove Primitive Baptist Church, Davidson County, North Carolina, Saturday, March 28, 1998. Recorded by Beverly Patterson.

18. #275, "On Jordan's stormy banks I stand" (C.M.)

Sung by Elder Johnny Ray and Wanda Naylor Gardner, Scarlette Kaye Gardner, Sylvia Snider, Doris Snider King, Connie Koontz, Delois and Paul Wilson, Ed and Donna White, Roy and Beatrice Pierce, Roy and Ethel Parrish, Gina Gobble, and Leonard Howard at Oak Grove Primitive Baptist Church, Davidson County, North Carolina, March 15, 1998. Recorded by Beverly Patterson.

Oak Grove Primitive Baptist Church is a branch of the Pine Primitive Baptist Church, about three miles away, from which it separated more than sixty years ago. Although it is independent, Oak Grove is in fellowship with a number of other Primitive Baptist churches that hold in common a belief in the absolute predestination of all things. On the last weekend in March, the church holds its three-day annual meeting, beginning Friday evening and ending Sunday afternoon. Primitive Baptist elders come here to preach not only from North Carolina, but also from Texas, Alabama, Louisiana, Virginia, West Virginia, California, Ohio, Michigan, and Mississippi. The meeting also draws visitors from New York, Georgia, Connecticut, and Oklahoma. Attendance at Oak Grove normally varies from about 45 to 60 people, but church clerk Sylvia Snider estimates that about 125 people attended the 1998 annual meeting.

"Come, we that love the Lord" was led by Elder Carl DuBose, visitng from the Little Hope Primitive Baptist Church, in Jasper, Texas. Under his leadership, the congregation transformed this eighteenth-century hymn by Isaac Watts into a camp-meeting style song, creating a full refrain, or chorus, from the last two lines of each stanza. Elder Johnny Ray Gardner can be heard singing the harmony. He said he learned the harmony part after hearing it sung by a woman at Little Hope when he was visiting there. "We call it the Texas tune," he says, "because we learned it there and brought it back here."

1 COME, we that love the Lord,
And let our joys be known,
Join in a song of sweet accord,
And thus surround the throne.

2 The sorrows of the mind
Be banished from this place;
Religion never was designed
To make our pleasures less.

3 Let those refuse to sing,
Who never knew our God;
But fav'rites of the heavenly King
May speak their joys abroad.

4 The hill of Zion yields
A thousand sacred sweets,
Before we reach the heavenly fields,
Or walk the golden streets.

5 Then let our songs abound,
And every tear be dry;
We're marching through Emmanuel's
To fairer world's on high. [ground

Services are held at Oak Grove on the third Sunday of each month and the Saturday evening before. On meeting Sundays, singing usually begins at the church about 10:30 a.m. and preaching at 11:00, followed by lunch, and often more singing, in the fellowship building where the following recording was made. Within its Primitive Baptist circles, the Oak Grove church has a well-deserved reputation for good singing. Elder Johnny Ray Gardner says he can lead the congregation in over one hundred tunes, all of them learned by ear and sung from memory, many of them sung in harmony. "When you learn songs by ear," he says, "it seems like it's easier than when you learn by note." The congregation usually sings from Benjamin Lloyd's *Primitive Hymns*, changing books only momentarily when someone requests a hymn from D. H. Goble's *The Primitive Baptist Hymn Book* (1887), a smaller collection of hymn texts.

Here members of the Oak Grove church, led by Doris Snider King, sing two verses of Samuel Stennett's eighteenth-century hymn, "On Jordan's stormy banks I stand," to a tune, "The Promised Land," that has been a favorite spiritual song for generations of Americans. That combination of hymn text and tune, with the added chorus "I am bound for the promised land," dates at least to 1835 when William Walker published it in his shape-note tunebook *The Southern Harmony*. Benjamin Lloyd published only

Stennett's hymn text in *The Primitive Hymns*. Singing from Lloyd's book, the congregation at Oak Grove spontaneously adds the familiar chorus, which most likely began as a camp meeting improvisation. These singers prefer singing the tune in a major key, a shift from its original publication in minor.

1 ON Jordan's stormy banks I stand,
And cast a wishful eye
To Canaan's fair and happy land,
Where my possessions lie.

2 O the transporting, rapt'rous scene,
That rises to my sight !
Sweet fields arrayed in living green,
And rivers of delight.

Bethel Primitive Baptist Church

19. #119, "Afflictions, though they seem severe" (C.M.)

Sung by Mr. and Mrs. Steve Woods, Mr. and Mrs. William Woods, Mr. and Mrs. Wendell Robertson, Mrs. and Mrs. Homer Benefield, Mrs. Jewel Baldwin, Mr. and Mrs. Kelton Williams, Beyrl Williams, Jeanette Brock, Mr. and Mrs. Ronald Gilmore, Mr. and Mrs. John Quick, Joe Green, Victor and Rhonda Quick, Ronnie Cobb, and Kenneth Fannin at Bethel Primitive Baptist Church, Berlin, Alabama, September 9, 1998. Recorded by Joyce Cauthen.

Elder Steve Woods gathered a group of people together to sing for this recording. It was not difficult to arrange as they already have a tradition of meeting once a month in various homes to eat together and sing hymns, some driving several hours to do so. Many of those present on this Wednesday evening at Bethel Primitive Baptist Church also sing from *The Sacred Harp, The Old School Hymnal,* and *The Good Old Songs.* Elder Woods, who led the singing, is the son of Elder William Woods, pastor of Bethel Church. He grew up singing only from Lloyd's hymn book. He prefers it to others because more of the hymns in it speak of free grace, which is the basis of the Primitive Baptist faith. He also finds the musical notation in other hymnals an unnecessary distraction, since he knows so many tunes by heart.

Elder Wendell Robertson also attends all of the singings, bringing a box of Lloyd's hymn books and a truckload of folding chairs when needed. He said that in his father's day, use of Lloyd's *Primitive Hymns* could be a test of fellowship. His church would not associate with those that used another hymn book, especially one with notes in it. "Folks felt that if the Lord didn't give you a tune, you're not supposed to sing it today." Now at gatherings such as this one, Primitive Baptists accustomed to singing from various hymn books fellowship together and enjoy the interchange of tunes, harmonies, repetitions of lines, and added choruses that others may bring to the texts in Lloyd.

The tune that Elder Woods used with #119, a common meter text written by John Newton, was suggested to him years ago by an elder from Winston County. In *The Sacred Harp* it is called "Columbus" and its meter is given as C.M.D. (common meter double), which means that two common meter verses are contained within the tune. The tune starts over again at the beginning of the third verse. Double common meter works particularly well with this text by John Newton telling the story of the "Prodigal Son."

1 AFFLICTIONS, though they seem severe,
In mercy oft are sent;
They stopped the prodigal's career,
And caused him to repent.

2 Although he no relentings felt,
Till he had spent his store,
His stubborn heart began to melt,
When famine pinched him sore.

3 'What have I gained by sin,' he said,
But hunger, shame and fear?
My father's house abounds with bread,
While I am starving here.

4 'I'll go and tell him all I've done,
And fall before his face;
Unworthy to be called his son,
I'll seek a servant's place.'

5 His father saw him coming back;
He saw, and ran and smiled,
And threw his arms around the neck
Of his repenting child.

6 'Father, I've sinned, but O forgive!'
'Enough,' the father said;
'Rejoice, my house, my son's alive,
For whom I mourned as dead.

7 'Now let the fatted calf be slain;
Go spread the news around;
My son was dead, but lives again,
Was lost, bnt now is found.'

8 'Tis thus the Lord his love reveals,
To call poor sinners home;
More than a father's love he feels,
And bids the needy come.

Bethlehem Primitive Baptist Church

20. #364, "Father, I stretch my hands to thee" (C.M.)

Sung by the congregation of Bethlehem Primitive Baptist Church, Eutaw, Alabama, May 12, 1996. Recorded by Joyce Cauthen.

Bethlehem Primitive Baptist Church sits on a hill overlooking the intersection of Interstate 59/20 and Highway 14, near Eutaw. Established in 1850, it is the mother church of the Sipsey River Association. It meets on the second Sunday of the month, thus its May footwashing service falls on Mother's Day each year. Many visitors attend church in honor of that day and to observe the moving communion and footwashing service.

This "Dr. Watts" style hymn was sung during the devotional period preceding the worship service. In the recording we hear the closing portion of a deacon's chant-like prayer. This prayer or the spirituality of the moment elicits a moan from a worshiper, who calls out, "Master, please come home, just a little while." Some members of the congregation join him as he repeats this phrase twice. The prayer ends quietly while another moan—"Want to feel your holy spirit"—begins. Then, without announcement, a hymn slowly emerges from the throat of a visiting elder, Frank Eatman, Jr., and the congregation takes it up and sings it with passion. The hymn by Charles Wesley is a familiar one that some line out from memory with the leader.

1 FATHER, I stretch my hands to thee,
No other help I know;
If thou withdraw thyself from me,
Ah! whither shall I go?

2 What did thine only Son endure
Before I drew my breath!
What pain, what labor, to secure
My soul from endless death!

See William Dargan's transcription of this performance of a moan followed by #364, "Father, I stretch my hands to thee," on pages 42–43 of this volume. See also Joyce Cauthen's essay on "Dr. Watts" hymns and the Sipsey River Association.

This CD was produced by Joyce Cauthen and digitally mastered by Philip Foster. Liner notes for Tracks 17 and 18 were written by Beverly Patterson, the rest by Joyce Cauthen in consultation with John Bealle, Joey Brackner, Beverly Patterson, William Dargan, Dan Patterson and Nicholas Temperley.

"Afflictions, though they seem severe" (#119): 111–12
African American churches: Primitive Baptist associations, 12; rise of independent churches, 11, 29
African American worship: African influences, 36; descent of the spirit, 16; devotional, 16, 36; frames, 12, 16; musical style synthesis, 29; preaching, 36; shouting, 16, 36, 38; Sipsey River Association, 12–18; Watts's importance, 3; *see also* moaning; ring shout; slavery
African Church of Mobile (Alabama): 31
African/European style synthesis: adaptation of printed melodies, 32, 33, 107; African tonal languages, 33, 38; basis for later forms, 37; attached choruses, 36–37; cultural tension, 31; emancipatory meaning of hymn texts, 36, 98; historical basis of, 29; lyrically measured speech, 35; percussive melody, 34; ring shout as "Methodist error," 36
Alabaha River Primitive Baptist Association (Georgia and Florida): 71
Allison, Jesse: 102–3, 104
"Amazing grace, how sweet the sound" (#3): adaptation of printed melody, 33; as "Dr. Watts" hymn, 7; as spiritual, 34; melismatic improvisation in, 14, 32; tempos, 103; text, 103; transcription, 41; melodies, 25, 103
Arminianism: 27, 58, 69
Atkins, A. V.: 70
Atkins, Mrs. "Mattie" E. (daughter-in-law of Benjamin Lloyd): 70, 71, 72, 77, 85

Baptist Church: in nineteenth century southern U.S., 60, 61; mission controversy, 2, 48–49, 51; relations with Anglicans in U.S., 58
Baptist Hymn Book (Beebe, 1858): 68
Baptist Hymn Book (Buck, 1842): 66
Beard's Creek Primitive Baptist Church (Georgia): 61
Beddome, Benjamin: 66
Beebe, Gilbert (*Baptist Hymn Book*, 1858): 68–69
Bell, Bertha: 103
Bell, Edward: 18, 104
"Beside the gospel pool" (#161): 16, 95
Bethel Primitive Baptist Church (Berlin, Alabama): 111–12
Bethlehem Primitive Baptist Church (New Site, Alabama) 96
Bethlehem Primitive Baptist Church (Eutaw, Alabama): 12, 113
Beulah Baptist Association (Alabama): 2, 48, 51, 52, 61, 68, 96
Black Creek Association: 73
Black Rock Address: 59
"Blessed be the tie that binds" (#196): 16, 18, 95
Bonar, Horatius: 34
Boyd, Josh and Rob: 104
Bradford, Sarah H.: 98
Brewer, George Evans: 53, 64
Broaddus, Andrew (*Dover Selection*, 1828): 65
Buchanan, President James: 64
Buck, William (*Baptist Hymn Book*, 1842): 66
Burdett, Staunton (*Baptist Hymnody*, 1834): 66

Calvin, John: 57, 58
camp meetings: 10–11, 109, 111
Cane Ridge: 10
Cayce, C. H. (*Good Old Songs*, 1913): 27, 71, 90, 93, 101
"A Charge to Keep I Have": 12
Cheatham, Peter: 69–70
choirs: introduction by reformers, 1, 9; Primitive Baptist views on, 24, 28; Shiloh Association, 98; Sipsey River Association, 12, 13, 104
choruses: attached, 25, 109, 111; camp meeting, 11, 109; improvised, 18, 28; printed in other books, 90, 99, 101, 110; "wandering," 34, 36
Christian Harmony (William Walker, 1866): 67, 90, 100
"The Christians of old, united in one" (#206): 75n62, 94, 97
Clark, Don: 73
Clarke, John (*Ebenezer Selection*), 1856): 69
Cockrell, Nellie: 12, 16
Collins, James: 18
Collins, Willie: 35
Columbus Association (Georgia): conservative views in, 2, 48, 60; joins Georgia State Convention, 49; Liberty Association and, 50
"Come, we that love the Lord" (#200): 109–10
Contentnea Association: 73
County Line Baptist Church (Alabama): 50, 61
Cowper, William: 66

Cox, Cary (father-in-law of Benjamin Lloyd): 60
Crawford, Richard: 32
Crawfordite Primitive Baptists: 92
Creek Indians: 18–19, 21n22
Crocker, Keith: 102
Crocker, Kevin: 102
Crocker, Latisha Smith: 102
Cusseta Church (Alabama): 50, 51, 61

Daily, John R. (*Primitive Baptist Hymn and Tune Book*, 1918): 27
"Dark and thorny is the desert" (#695): as emancipatory text, 98; origin of melody used, 32; percussive melody, 33, 34, 35; shout-like performance of, 34; text, 99; transcription, 44
Davies, Samuel: 10, 36
"The day is past and gone" (#440): "Dr. Watts" hymn, 7; freely measured speech rhythms, 34; melismatic improvisation, 33; melody used, 16, 31–32, 95; text, 95; transcription, 40
Dean, Bufrey: 96
Deason family: 100, 102
Dett, R. Nathaniel: 33
devotional: 16, 36
"Did Christ the great example lead" (#258): 18, 75n62
Doddridge, Phillip: 66, 67
Dorsey, Thomas: 38
Dossey, William (*Dossey's Choice*, 1830): 65, 67
Dover Selection (Broaddus, 1828): 65
"Dr. Watts" hymn singing: decline, 12, 14, 18; description, 7, 14; in Sipsey River Association, 14–18, 104; John Wesley Work on, 32–33; origins of melodies, 8; printed tunes avoided, 8; scope of term, 7; tempos, 103, 107
Drummond, Paul: 59, 73
DuBois, W. E. B.: 37
DuBose, Carl: 109
Dupuy, Starke (*Hymns and Spiritual Songs*, 1818): 65
Durand, Silas H. (*Hymn and Tune Book*, 1886): 26–27

Eatman, Frank, Jr.: 15, 95, 113
Ebenezer Baptist Association (Alabama): 51
Ebenezer Selection of Hymns and Spiritual Songs (Clarke, 1856): 69
English Particular Baptists: 23
Epstein, Dena: 32, 36, 37
"Father, I stretch my hands to thee" (#364): "Dr. Watts hymn," 7; freely measured speech rhythms, 34; melismatic improvisation, 33; melody, 32; preceded by moaning, 15–16, 35, 42, 113; text, 113; transcription, 42–43
Fawcett, John: 66
fellowshipping: 14–15, 33, 106–7
Flint River Association: 48
Floyd, Samuel: 32
footwashing: 14, 17–19, 113
Fort Dale Primitive Baptist Church (Alabama): 52
Franklin, James (Jeoffery Chanticleer): 9
"From every stormy wind that blows" (#333): 67, 105–6

Gardner, Johnny Ray: 109–10
"Geneva Jigs": 8
Georgia Baptist Convention: 49, 60
"Go down, Moses": 34
Goble, D. H. (*Primitive Baptist Hymn Book*, 1887): 25, 26, 110
Good Old Songs (Cayce, 1913): 27, 71, 90, 93, 101
Goodwill Association (Alabama): 104
gospel music: 12, 37
Granbury, Thomas: 49
Gray, John M.: 49, 54n9, 60
Great Awakening (First): 1, 29
Great Awakening (Second): 9, 10, 36

Hall, Vera: 102–3
"Hark the voice of love and mercy" (#49): 18
harmony: in New England psalmody, 9; in Primitive Baptist singing, 24, 27, 92, 105, 109–10
Harris, Michael: 38
Hawker, Annie Maude: 105
Hawker, Ginny: 105–6
High, Willie B.: 30
High Bluff Primitive Baptist Church (Hoboken, Georgia): 92
Hillabee Association (Alabama): 96–97
Holcombe, Hosea: 60, 61
Houser, Margaret: 98
Houser, Ronnie: 98–99
"Hungry, and faint, and poor" (#492): 95, 100–101
Hymn and Tune Book (Durand and Lester, 1886): 26–27
hymnody: accessibility of, 9–10; homiletical function, 57–58; modernism and, 1, 37; personal spirituality and, 1; revival choruses, 11, 109
Hymns and Spiritual Songs (Dupuy, 1818): 65

"I walked abroad one morning fair" (#152): 94
"I would, but cannot sing" (#390): 96–97
"Idumea": 31, 95, 100, 108
"invisible churches": 11

Jackson, George Pullen: on lining-out, 7–8; on origin of spirituals, 31, 32; on sources for Primitive Hymns, 67, 93, 101, 103
"Jesus is a rock in a weary land": 34
Jones, Charles Colcock: 11

Kehukee Association: 73
Kehukee Declaration: 59
Kentucky Harmony (1815): 100
King, Doris Snider: 110
Krehbiel, Henry: 37

LaFayette Baptist Church (Alabama): 51, 61
Lee, Clarke: 73, 92
Lee, David: 73, 91–93
Lee family: 73, 91–94, 97
Lee, Kathy: 93
Leland, John: 59, 95
Lester, P. G. (*Hymn and Tune Book*, 1886): 26–27
Liberty Baptist Association (Alabama): 51, 61
lining out: among Missionary Baptists, 37; Cotton Mather on, 8; decline of, 73, 108; defined, 3, 24; European roots, 8, 59; in Sipsey River Association, 14–16, 104; Isaac Watts on, 10; John Rippon on, 59; post-Reconstruction era, 37; sanctioned by Westminster Assembly, 8; *see also* "Dr. Watts" hymn singing; "old way of singing"; Primitive Baptist singing
Little Hope Primitive Baptist Church (Eoline, Alabama): 23, 100–102
Little Hope Primitive Baptist Church (Jasper, Texas): 109
Lloyd, Benjamin: birth and childhood, 48; relocation to Alabama, 50; ministerial pursuits, 48, 50, 51, 52; professional pursuits, 48, 50, 52, 60–61, 62, 63; "the Palings" (Lloyd plantation and family cemetery), 49, 52, 63, 64; views on the church, 48–49, 53; death, 53, 64
Lloyd, Cary Chappell (second son): 50
Lloyd, Francis Bartow (grandson, pseud. "Rufus Sanders"): 52
Lloyd, Jesse Cox (tenth son): 70
Lloyd, John E., Sr. (father): 48, 54n3, 55n21
Lloyd, John Franklyn (eldest son): 48, 63
Lloyd, John (grandfather): 54n3
Lloyd, Joseph (brother): 50
Lloyd, Joseph LaFayette (third son): 50
Lloyd, Martha "Mattie" (daughter-in-law): *see* Atkins, Mrs. "Mattie" E.
Lloyd, Naomi Ann Cox (wife): 48, 64, 69–70
Lomax, John A. and Ruby T.: 102–3
Lovell, John: 37
Lower Wetumpka Association (Alabama): 96

Manley, Basil: 59
Martin, Mable: 105
mascons (mass concentration of meaning): 34
Mather, Cotton: 8
McGinty, B. B. (*History of the East Liberty Baptist Association*, 1963): 51
melisma: "poetic rhythms" as basis for, 35; style tension with prevailing rhythm, 32–33, 38
melody: adaptation of printed sources, 31–32, 92; avoidance of printed sources, 8, 111; description by Nellie Cockrell, 16; divinely inspired, 73–74, 100, 108, 111; "Dr. Watts" melodies, 8, 32; New England psalmody, 9; percussive vs. lyrical, 34; Primitive Baptist melodies, 25, 90; suggested by Lloyd, 67; unprinted melodies, 25, 67, 75–76n62, 94; variation among churches, 27
Mercer, Jesse (*Mercer's Cluster*): 59, 61, 65, 66, 67
"Mercy Seat": *see* "From every stormy wind that blows" (#333)
meter: abbreviations, 91, 112; freely measured speech rhythms, 34–35; iambic rhythm flow, 34; memorization and quatrain form, 11–12; Psalms adapted to, 16; Sipsey River practice, 16; strictly measured speech rhythms, 35
"Mixtures of joy and sorrow" (#384): 25
moaning: described, 15–16, 113; importance in African American churches, 36; measured speech rhythms and, 34–35, 38; source of "blue notes," 46n11; *see also* African American worship
Monsees, J. A. (*Old School Hymnal*): 27, 90
Moody, Dwight (*Sacred Songs and Solos with Standard Hymns*): 11

Mount Hebrew Primitive Baptist Church (Notasulga, Alabama): 16, 108–9
Mount Pilgrim Primitive Baptist Church (Livingston, Alabama): 18, 30, 103, 104
Mount Pisgah Baptist Church (Bibb County, Georgia): 48
Mount Pisgah Baptist Church (Stroud, Alabama): 66
Mount Zion Primitive Baptist Church (Butler County, Alabama): 52, 96
Music, David W.: 9
musical instruments: advocated by reformers 9; Calvinist views on, 59; in African American churches, 12; in Primitive Baptist churches, 24, 59, 98, 104, 108

Nettleton, Asahel (*Village Hymns,* 1824): 67
"New Britain": *see* "Amazing Grace, how sweet the sound" (#3): melodies
New Jerusalem Primitive Baptist Church (Bessemer, Alabama): 95
Newton, John: 33–34, 66, 96, 100, 103, 112
Norton, Kay: 66

"O land of rest for thee I sigh" (#689): 25, 71
"O may I worthy prove to see" (#270): 31, 33, 99
Oak Grove Primitive Baptist Church (Davidson County, North Carolina): 109–11
Oak Grove Primitive Baptist Church (Sylacauga, Alabama): 96
Old Mill Primitive Baptist Church: 105
Old School Hymnal: 27, 90, 101
Old School Primitive Baptist Association: 12
Old School Sonnets (Osborn, 1836): 65–66
"old way of singing": current distribution in U.S., 18–19, 21n22; introduction in southern U.S., 57; introduction in U.S., 8; *see also* lining out
"On Jordan's stormy banks I stand" (#275): 110–11
Original Sipsey River Association: *see* Sipsey River Association
Osbourn, James (*Old School Sonnets,* 1836): 65–66
particular atonement: 58
Patterson, Daniel: 46n5
Peterson, Thomas: 108
Philadelphia Baptist Association: 23
Pinckney, Charles Cotesworth: 11
Pine Primitive Baptist Church (Davidson County, North Carolina): 109
"Pisgah": 103
Pitts, Walter F., Jr.: 12, 16, 34–35, 36
"poetic rhythms": 35
"portraiture sound": 35
"praise houses": 11
predestination: 14, 23, 58, 66, 101
Primitive Baptist Church: adoption of "Primitive" name, 23; architecture, 13, 23–24; associations, 2, 13, 91; core beliefs, 2, 22–23, 57, 58, 98, 104; founding of, 23, 59; opposition to centralized authority, 22–24, 27, 58–59, 69; position on missions, 2, 23, 48–49, 51; profile of members, 13, 22; religious identity, 26, 28; role of women, 13, 24, 98, 108; *see also* Baptist Church; Primitive Baptist singing
Primitive Baptist Hymn and Tune Book (Daily, 1918): 27
Primitive Baptist Hymn Book (Goble, 1887): 25, 26, 110
Primitive Baptist singing: African/European style synthesis, 29; alteration of texts, 35, 69, 97, 101; books used, 13, 25, 26–27; differences in style, 27–28; factors in choosing texts, 25, 69; harmony, 24, 27, 92, 105, 109–10; musical instruments, 12, 24, 59, 98, 104, 108; song leaders, 28, 109; sound as central concern, 2, 25–26, 28; spirituality in, 59, 73–74, 90, 108; tempo, 24, 108; *see also* choirs; fellowshipping; lining out; "raising a hymn"
Primitive Hymns: first edition (1841), 2, 52, 57, 62–63, 67, 78–79; third edition (1845), 65, 67, 80–81; 1906 edition, 85, 92; frontispiece, 60; preface, 77; subject references, 1, 57–58, 62, 66, 77, 78–79, 82; sources of texts, 65–67, 75n52; theology of texts, 25, 27, 65, 66, 68–69, 75n50, 97, 101, 111; provisions in Lloyd will for publication, 53, 64, 69; sales, 67, 72–73, 76n82
Primitive Hymns Corporation: vi, 72–73, 76n82, 87
"Promised Land, The": *see* "On Jordan's stormy banks I stand" (#275)
psalmody: 8–10

"raising a hymn": 15, 74, 100, 104
Reed, Doc: 102–3
Reeves, Philip: 92
regular singing: 9, 59

revival hymnody: 9
ring shout: 33, 35, 36, 46n12; *see also* African American worship; shouting
Rippon, John (*Selection of Hymns*, 1787): 59, 65, 66, 67
Robertson, Wendell: 111
"Romish Lady, The": *see* "There was a Romish lady, brought up in Popery" (#698)

Sacred Harp: 31–32, 57, 73, 90, 91–93, 96, 112
Sacred Songs and Solos with Standard Hymns (Sankey and Moody): 11
salvation by grace: 14, 22, 23, 25, 36, 57
Sanders, Rufus: *see* Lloyd, Francis Bartow
Sankey, Ira (*Sacred Songs and Solos with Standard Hymns*): 11
"Saw ye my Savior" (#45): 93
Seeger, Ruth Crawford: 32
Seven Miles Association: 73
Shiloh Primitive Baptist Association (North Carolina): 35, 98–100
Shiloh Primitive Baptist Church (Elkin, North Carolina): 98
shouting: 16, 36, 38, 46n12; *see also* African American worship; ring shout
singing schools: 59
Sipsey River Association (Alabama and Michigan): architecture, 13; Articles of Faith, 14; founding, 12–13; member churches, 13, 95, 104, 113; worship practices, 13, 14–18
slavery: Christianization movement, 11; conversion experiences, 10; Emancipation, 11, 37; Great Awakening (First), 29; "invisible churches," 10; "praise houses," 11; *see also* African American worship
Smith, Amanda: 31, 106–7
Smith, Clara Deason: 102
Smith, Donald: 69, 72, 74, 100, 102
Smith, La Verte Lloyd (granddaughter): 72–73, 85–87
Smitherman, Geneva: 33
Smyrna Primitive Baptist Church (Goodwater, Alabama): 94, 96–97
Smyth, Willie: 21n22
Snider, Sylvia: 109
Sobel, Mechal: 29–31
"songified speech": 33
songsters: 10–11
Southern, Eileen: 32
Southern Harmony (William Walker, 1835): 110
spirituals: hymn texts and, 34, 36; origin controversy, 31, 32, 37, 38; W. E. B. DuBois on, 37
Spring Hill Union Association (Alabama): 11, 106–7, 108
Stearns, Shubal: 10
Steele, Anne: 66
Stennett, Samuel: 110–11
Stowell, Hugh: 106
Stuckey, Sterling: 36
surge songs: 7
"Sweet to rejoice in lively hope" (#662): 101
Symmes, Rev. Thomas: 9

Tartt, Ruby Pickens: 102–3
Temperley, Nicholas: 8, 9
Tennyson, Don: 66, 69, 73
Terry, Opal Lloyd (granddaughter of Benjamin Lloyd): 72, 85–87
"That doleful night before his death" (#241): "Dr. Watts" hymn, 7; freely measured speech rhythms, 34, 35; melismatic improvisation, 33; sung preceding communion, 17, 104; text, 104; transcription, 45
"There was a Romish lady, brought up in Popery" (#698): 70, 71–72, 76n75, 77, 83–85
True Faith Primitive Baptist Church (Winston-Salem, North Carolina): 98
Tubman, Harriet: 98
tunebooks: 28, 59, 67, 90
"Twas on that dark and doleful night" (#240): 17

Village Hymns (Nettleton, 1824): 67

Walker, Wyatt Tee: 11–12
Walter, Rev. Thomas: 9
wandering chorus: 34, 36
Washington, Booker T.: 37
Watson, Rev. John: 36
Watts, Isaac: accessibility of Watts's hymns, 9–10; African Americans and, 3; homiletical hymnody, 57; *Hymns and Spiritual Songs*, 9, 10; opinion of lining out, 10; in Primitive Hymns, 66, 67; *see also* "Dr. Watts" singing
"Wayfaring Stranger": 25
Welsh Tract Church: 23
Wesley, Charles: 66, 113
Wesley, John: 10, 36, 66, 67
Wesley, Samuel: 66
Westminster Assembly: 8
Wetumpka Association (Alabama): 52

"What wondrous love is this" (#263): adaptation of printed source, 33, 38; lyrical melody for, 31, 34; text, 107; transcription, 39
"While sorrows encompass me round" (#382): adaptation of printed source, 33; text, 108–9; transcription, 44; melody not in tunebooks, 75n62
White, Ella Pearl: 31, 106–7
Whitefield, George: 10, 36
Whitfield, Lieutenant: 104
Whittington, Gail: 98
"Wondrous Love": *see* "What wondrous love is this" (#263)
Woodard, Bettie: 76n82
Woods, Steve: 111–12
Woods, William: 111
Work, John Wesley: 32–33, 35, 38
Wyers, Douglas: 102
Wyeth John (*Repository of Sacred Music*, 1810): 67

"Ye objects of sense, and enjoyments of time" (#595): 93

BENJAMIN LLOYD'S HYMN BOOK: A PRIMITIVE BAPTIST SONG TRADITION

Lee family, Hoboken, Georgia
1. #595, "Ye objects of sense, and enjoyments of time" (1:22)
2. #45, "Saw ye my Savior" (2:00)
3. #152, "I walked abroad one morning fair" (1:30)
4. #206, "The Christians of old, united in one" (1:19)

New Jerusalem Primitive Baptist Church, Bessemer, Alabama
5. #440, "The day is past and gone" (5:01)

Smyrna Primitive Baptist Church, Goodwater, Alabama
6. #390, "I would, but cannot sing" (3:09)
7. #206, "The Christians old, united in one" (4:13)

Shiloh Primitive Baptist Association, Elkin, North Carolina
8. #695, "Dark and thorny is the desert" (5:27)
9. #270, "O may I worthy prove to see" (4:07)

Little Hope Primitive Baptist Church, Eoline, Alabama
10. #492, "Hungry, and faint, and poor" (1:52)
11. #662, "Sweet to rejoice in lively hope" (4:42)

Jesse Allison, Doc Reed, and Vera Hall, Livingston, Alabama
12. #3, "Amazing grace, how sweet the sound" (2:38)

Mt. Pilgrim Primitive Baptist Church, Livingston, Alabama
13. #241, "That doleful night before his death" (2:54)

Ginny Hawker, Augusta Heritage Center, Davis and Elkins College, Elkins, West Virginia
14. #333, "From every stormy wind that blows" (4:28)

Amanda Smith and Ella Pearl White, Loachapoka, Alabama
15. #263, "What wondrous love is this" (3:14)

Mt. Hebrew Primitive Baptist Church, Notasulaga, Alabama
16. #382, "While sorrows encompass me round" (5:08)

Oak Grove Primitive Baptist Church, Davidson County, North Carolina
17. #200, "Come, we that love the Lord" (4:48)
18. #275, "On Jordan's stormy banks I stand" (2:13)

Bethel Primitive Baptist Church, Berlin, Alabama
19. #119, "Afflictions, though they seem severe" (2:43)

Bethlehem Primitive Baptist Church, Eutaw, Alabama
20. #364, "Father, I stretch my hands to thee" (7:22)

See complete notes to these performances in accompanying essay collection.